MOVIE ★ ICONS

GARBO

EDITOR
PAUL DUNCAN

TEXT
DAVID ROBINSON

PHOTOS
THE KOBAL COLLECTION

TASCHEN

HONG KONG KÖLN LONDON LOS ANGELES MADRID PARIS TOKYO

CONTENTS

8

GRETA GARBO: DIVINE
14 GRETA GARBO: DIE GÖTTLICHE
18 GRETA GARBO : LA DIVINE
by David Robinson

22

VISUAL FILMOGRAPHY
22 FILMOGRAFIE IN BILDERN
22 FILMOGRAPHIE EN IMAGES

178

CHRONOLOGY
182 CHRONOLOGIE
184 CHRONOLOGIE

186

FILMOGRAPHY
186 FILMOGRAFIE
186 FILMOGRAPHIE

192

BIBLIOGRAPHY
192 BIBLIOGRAFIE
192 BIBLIOGRAPHIE

1

GRETA GARBO: DIVINE

BY DAVID ROBINSON

GRETA GARBO: DIE GÖTTLICHE

GRETA GARBO: LA DIVINE

GRETA GARBO: DIVINE

by David Robinson

Greta Garbo's beauty is timeless. She was uniquely photogenic, and her performances in *Queen Christina* (1933) and *Camille* (1936) would be enough to establish her as one of the cinema's greatest actresses. A hint of a smile, a touch or a glance can intimate the utmost depths of human thought, feeling, being. She was languid, distant, melancholy; and yet in love scenes she conveyed a passion and hunger that startled audiences and overturned American notions of eroticism. Part of her fascination, too, was the mystery of her private life and loves: "I want to be left alone," she insisted; and no one ever really knew her. This child of a poor Stockholm working family was destined to become and remains the world's divine woman.

Greta Lovisa Gustafsson was born on 18 September 1905 in Stockholm. Leaving school, she worked briefly as a barber's lather girl, a precocious experience of tactile encounter with the opposite sex. As a department store apprentice she was chosen to appear in a couple of publicity films. Fired with the ambition to act, she won a scholarship to the Royal Dramatic Theatre Academy, and had a couple of small film roles before being cast in *Gösta Berlings saga* (*The Atonement of Gosta Berling*, 1924) by the outstanding director Mauritz Stiller, who renamed her Garbo. Her exceptional screen presence was immediately apparent. G. W. Pabst gave her a role in the German production *Die freudlose Gasse* (*The Joyless Street*, 1925), and meanwhile Louis B. Mayer offered Stiller and Garbo contracts to work for MGM in Hollywood, where they arrived in September 1924. Stiller's autocratic and idiosyncratic methods did not suit the studio. He was removed from direction of Garbo's second film, *The Temptress* (1926), and in 1927 returned to Stockholm, where he died the following year aged 45, depriving Garbo of her crucial formative influence.

She made ten films in the last golden age of silent cinema. Few, except *Flesh and the Devil* (1927), *Love* (1927, from Tolstoy's *Anna Karenina*) and *The Kiss* (1929), were notable in

PORTRAIT FOR 'GRAND HOTEL' (1932)

"Life would be so wonderful if we only knew what to do with it."
Greta Garbo

themselves; yet, phenomenally, Garbo's performances gave reality and richness even to the least worthy vehicles, turning novelettes into something like art. She was big box office as well. In 1930 MGM boasted 'Garbo Talks!' and *Anna Christie* revealed a sultry voice as fascinating as her looks. She was now MGM's most valuable asset, and the company invested extravagantly in productions that rarely merited what she brought to them. One of the exceptions was the all-star *Grand Hotel* (1932). Finally, working with superior directors, she made a trilogy of great costume dramas, Rouben Mamoulian's *Queen Christina* (1933), Clarence Brown's *Anna Karenina* (1935) and George Cukor's *Camille* (1937). Ironically, as her films reached this apogee, her public began to drop away – at least in America: in Europe she continued to reign supreme, until World War Two closed markets.

In Ernst Lubitsch's *Ninotchka* (1939), as the publicity declared, 'Garbo Laughs!' She displayed new vitality and a natural gift for comedy. MGM's follow-up, *Two-Faced Woman* (1941), however, was a disaster. Garbo received her first bad notices, and never made another film. From time to time there were rumours of a comeback and even, in 1949, film tests. But Garbo withdrew from public view. She died on 15 April 1990, and in 1999 her ashes were transferred, with national ceremony, to Skogskyrkogården cemetery in her native Stockholm.

What was the secret of Garbo? The beauty was unique and irresistible to the camera: her favourite cameraman, William Daniels, said it was impossible to light her unflatteringly. The deep voice, the distinctive walk and posture, at once languid and powerful, added to the glamour. She had a unique eroticism, perhaps powered by her own ambiguous and eventful private emotional life. In love scenes, she is always, subtly, the dominant partner.

Finally, though, she was a truly great actress. She hid her secrets. She would not rehearse; her set was screened so that no-one could distract her; sometimes even the director was excluded. Yet she came to the set word perfect, and incapable of making a false move. In all other respects apparently lethargic, she was deeply serious about her art, and obdurate in demanding the right conditions for it. One can only guess that the uncompromising Stiller had instilled in her a regime of meticulous rehearsal and preparation in the long hours of her secret private life, which, when added to her flawless instinct and innate gifts, resulted in her sublime presence on the silver screen.

ENDPAPERS/VOR- UND NACHSATZBLÄTTER/
PAGES DE GARDE
PORTRAITS FOR 'THE TEMPTRESS' (1926)

PAGES 2/3
STILL FROM 'FLESH AND THE DEVIL' (1927)

PAGE 4
PORTRAIT FOR 'LOVE' (1927)

PAGES 6/7
ON THE SET OF 'ANNA KARENINA' (1935)

PAGE 8
PORTRAIT FOR 'MATA HARI' (1931)

OPPOSITE/RECHTS/CI-CONTRE
PORTRAIT (JULY 1925)

GRETA GARBO:
DIE GÖTTLICHE

von David Robinson

Greta Garbos Schönheit ist zeitlos. Die Schwedin war einzigartig fotogen, und allein ihre Auftritte in *Königin Christine* (1933) und *Die Kameliendame* (1936) würden ausreichen, um sie als eine der größten Filmschauspielerinnen zu etablieren. Nur durch den Anflug eines Lächelns, durch eine Berührung oder einen Blick konnte sie die größten Tiefen menschlichen Denkens, Fühlens und Seins andeuten. Sie galt als träge, distanziert und melancholisch, aber in Liebesszenen begeisterte sie das Publikum mit ihrer Leidenschaft und stellte die Ideen der Amerikaner von Erotik auf den Kopf. Einer der Gründe für die Faszination, die von ihr ausging, war sicherlich das Geheimnis, das ihr Privat- und Liebesleben umgab: Sie bestand darauf, allein gelassen zu werden, und niemand kannte die wahre Garbo. Diese Tochter einer armen Stockholmer Arbeiterfamilie war auserkoren, „die Göttliche" zu spielen, und für ihr Publikum ist sie es bis heute geblieben.

Greta Lovisa Gustafsson wurde am 18. September 1905 in Stockholm geboren. Nach ihrer Schulzeit arbeitete sie für kurze Zeit als Einseiferin bei einem Barbier und sammelte so schon früh erste Erfahrungen mit der Berührung des anderen Geschlechts. Danach begann sie eine Lehre in einem Warenhaus und spielte in einigen Werbefilmchen mit. Ihr schauspielerischer Ehrgeiz war geweckt, sie erhielt ein Stipendium für die Schauspielschule des Königlichen Dramatischen Theaters in Stockholm und hatte einige kleinere Auftritte, bevor man ihr eine Hauptrolle in *Gösta Berling* (1924) unter der Regie des großen Mauritz Stiller anbot. Ihm verdankt sie auch ihren Künstlernamen Garbo. Sofort fiel ihre außergewöhnliche Präsenz auf der Leinwand auf. G. W. Pabst besetzte sie in dem deutschen Stummfilm *Die freudlose Gasse* (1925). Gleichzeitig unterbreitete Louis B. Mayer ihr und Stiller einen Vertrag mit MGM in Hollywood, wo beide schließlich im September 1924 eintrafen. Stillers eigensinnige und selbstherrliche Art passte dem Studio jedoch nicht, und man entzog ihm die Regie bereits bei Garbos zweitem amerikanischen Film, *Dämon Weib*. Daraufhin kehrte er 1927 nach Stockholm zurück, wo er im Jahr darauf im Alter von nur 45 Jahren starb. Damit verlor Garbo den Menschen, der ihren Werdegang entscheidend geprägt hatte.

PORTRAIT FOR 'WILD ORCHIDS' (1929)

„Das Leben wäre so wunderbar, wenn wir nur etwas damit anzufangen wüssten."
Greta Garbo

In den letzten goldenen Jahren des Stummfilms drehte Greta Garbo zehn Filme. Nur wenige von ihnen – darunter *Es war* (1927), *Anna Karenina* (1927, nach Tolstois Romanepos) und *Der Kuß* (1929) – waren an sich bemerkenswert, doch Garbos Schauspielkunst war phänomenal, bereicherte selbst den trivialsten Streifen und verwandelte jedes Dramolett in ein wahres Kunstwerk. Auch ihr Kassenerfolg konnte sich sehen lassen. 1930 verkündete MGM: „Die Garbo spricht!", und *Anna Christie* enthüllte eine heißblütige Stimme, die ebenso faszinierend war wie ihr Äußeres. Sie wurde zu MGMs wertvollstem Kapital, und das Studio investierte Riesensummen in Produktionen, die ihr Mitwirken eigentlich nicht verdienten. Eine rühmliche Ausnahme war der mit vielen Stars besetzte Film *Menschen im Hotel* (1932). Schließlich drehte sie unter erstklassigen Regisseuren eine Trilogie großer Kostümfilme: Rouben Mamoulians *Königin Christine* (1933), Clarence Browns *Anna Karenina* (1935) und George Cukors *Die Kameliendame* (1936). Ironischerweise begann das amerikanische Publikum ihr auf dem qualitativen Höhepunkt ihrer Karriere den Rücken zu kehren; in Europa jedoch hielt ihr Ruhm an, bis der Zweite Weltkrieg den kontinentalen Markt abschnitt.

In Ernst Lubitschs *Ninotschka* (1939) lachte Garbo sogar, wie die Filmwerbung hervorhob: Sie stellte eine bisher unbekannte Lebhaftigkeit und eine natürliche Begabung für Komik zur Schau. Das nächste MGM-Projekt, *Die Frau mit den zwei Gesichtern*, entpuppte sich jedoch als Desaster, und Greta Garbo erhielt erstmals schlechte Kritiken. Danach drehte sie nie wieder einen Film. Von Zeit zu Zeit gab es Gerüchte über ein Comeback und 1949 sogar einige Kameraproben. Aber Garbo zog sich ganz aus der Öffentlichkeit zurück. Sie starb am 15. April 1990, und 1999 wurde ihre Asche feierlich auf den Friedhof Skogskyrkogården ihrer Geburtsstadt Stockholm überführt.

Was war das Geheimnis der Garbo? Ihre Schönheit war einzigartig und für die Kamera unwiderstehlich: Ihr Lieblingskameramann, William Daniels, sagte einmal, es sei unmöglich, sie nicht schmeichelhaft auszuleuchten. Ihre tiefe Stimme, ihr charakteristischer Gang und ihre typische Pose – behäbig und zugleich kraftvoll – steigerten ihren Zauber nur noch. Sie besaß eine einmalige erotische Ausstrahlung, deren Antriebskraft möglicherweise in ihrem undurchsichtigen und ereignisreichen Privatleben zu finden war. In Liebesszenen war sie auf subtile Weise stets die dominante Kraft.

Und schließlich war sie eine großartige Schauspielerin. Sie behielt ihr Geheimnis für sich. Sie probte nicht. Das Set wurde vorher abgesucht, damit sie durch nichts abgelenkt wurde. Manchmal musste sogar der Regisseur draußen bleiben. Trotzdem erschien sie perfekt vorbereitet zu den Dreharbeiten, und jede Bewegung saß. Obgleich sie in jeder anderen Hinsicht lethargisch wirkte, nahm sie ihre Kunst äußerst ernst und kannte keine Kompromisse, wenn es darum ging, die passenden Voraussetzungen dafür zu schaffen. Man kann nur mutmaßen, dass ihr der unnachgiebige Stiller in den langen Stunden ihres geheimen Privatlebens die äußerst sorgfältige Vorbereitung beigebracht hatte, die sich mit ihrem untrüglichen Instinkt und ihrer angeborenen Begabung zu einer alles überstrahlenden Präsenz auf der Leinwand vereinte.

COVER FOR 'MOTION PICTURE' (MARCH 1929)

Motion Picture

MARCH   25 CENTS

THE STARS WHO STAND OUT
THERE'S NO PANIC IN HOLLYWOOD
and 18 Other Hot Features

GRETA GARBO : LA DIVINE

David Robinson

La beauté de Greta Garbo est intemporelle. Extraordinairement photogénique, elle aurait pu se contenter de *La Reine Christine* (1933) et du *Roman de Marguerite Gautier* (1936) pour s'imposer comme une des plus grandes actrices de l'histoire du cinéma. L'ébauche d'un sourire, d'un geste ou d'un regard lui suffit pour sonder les profondeurs de la nature humaine. D'ordinaire alanguie, distante et mélancolique, elle laisse s'exprimer dans les scènes d'amour une passion avide qui désarçonne le public et bouleverse la conception américaine de l'érotisme. La fascination qu'elle inspire découle également du mystère qui entoure sa vie privée et sentimentale. « Laissez-moi seule », répète inlassablement celle qui demeurera toujours une inconnue, cette fille d'une modeste famille suédoise destinée à devenir la Divine aux yeux de la postérité.

Greta Lovisa Gustafsson est née le 18 septembre 1905 à Stockholm. À 14 ans, elle travaille chez un barbier, expérience précoce des contacts physiques avec le sexe opposé. Devenue vendeuse dans un grand magasin, elle est choisie pour jouer dans quelques films publicitaires. Poussée par l'ambition de devenir comédienne, elle obtient une bourse à l'Académie royale d'art dramatique et décroche de petits rôles dans des films avant de tourner *La Légende de Gösta Berling* (1924) avec le grand réalisateur suédois Mauritz Stiller, qui la rebaptise Greta Garbo. Elle se fait immédiatement remarquer par son exceptionnelle présence à l'écran. G. W. Pabst lui confie un rôle dans le film allemand *La Rue sans joie* (1925). De son côté, Louis B. Mayer propose à Stiller et Garbo des contrats avec la MGM à Hollywood, où ils débarquent en 1924. Mais les méthodes inhabituelles et autocratiques de Stiller ne conviennent pas à la MGM. Après s'être vu retirer la réalisation du deuxième film de Garbo, *La Tentatrice* (1926), Stiller retourne à Stockholm en 1927. Il y meurt l'année suivante à l'âge de 45 ans, privant l'actrice de son influence si formatrice.

Garbo tourne dix films à la fin de l'âge d'or du cinéma muet. Hormis *La Chair et le Diable* (1927), *Anna Karénine* (1927, d'après le roman de Tolstoï) et *Le Baiser* (1929), ces films n'ont guère d'intérêt en eux-mêmes. Mais le jeu de l'actrice confère aux supports les plus médiocres un réalisme et une richesse qui transforment des romans de quatre sous en véritables œuvres d'art. Un talent qui fait le bonheur du box-office. En 1930, à grand renfort de publicités annonçant que

PORTRAIT (1931)
Garbo roared with laughter when she saw this composite picture by Clarence Sinclair Bull. / Greta Garbo schüttelte sich vor Lachen, als sie diese Fotomontage von Clarence Sinclair Bull sah. / En découvrant ce photo-montage de Clarence Sinclair Bull, Garbo éclate de rire.

« La vie serait si merveilleuse si on savait quoi en faire. »
Greta Garbo

«Garbo parle!», *Anna Christie* révèle une voix sensuelle, aussi captivante que son visage. Garbo devient l'atout le plus précieux de la MGM, qui investit des sommes colossales dans des films rarement à la hauteur du talent de la star. L'une des rares exceptions est *Grand Hôtel* (1932), où elle est entourée d'une pléiade de vedettes. Enfin, grâce à des réalisateurs de haut niveau, Garbo tourne une trilogie de grands films historiques, *La Reine Christine* (1933) de Rouben Mamoulian, *Anna Karénine* (1935) de Clarence Brown et *Le Roman de Marguerite Gautier* (1937) de George Cukor. L'ironie du sort veut qu'au moment même où sa carrière atteint son apogée, son public commence à se détourner d'elle en Amérique. En Europe, elle demeure indétrônable jusqu'à la Seconde Guerre mondiale.

En 1939, le slogan qui annonce la sortie de *Ninotchka* d'Ernst Lubitsch marque un nouveau tournant: «Garbo rit!». L'actrice y fait preuve d'une vitalité insoupçonnée et d'un don naturel pour la comédie. Hélas, elle tourne ensuite *La Femme aux deux visages* (1941), qui sera un véritable désastre. Ce film, qui lui vaut pour la première fois d'être éreintée par la critique, sonne le glas de sa carrière. Des rumeurs annoncent de temps à autre son come-back. En 1949, elle tourne même quelques bouts d'essai. Mais la star se retire de la vie publique. Elle meurt le 15 avril 1990 et en 1999, ses cendres sont transférées avec les honneurs nationaux au cimetière Skogskyrkogården de Stockholm, sa ville natale.

Quel est le secret de Garbo? Sa beauté inégalée semble irrésistiblement attirer la caméra: son chef opérateur favori, William Daniels, déclare qu'il est impossible de l'éclairer de manière peu flatteuse. Sa voix profonde, sa démarche et sa posture si particulières, à la fois alanguies et puissantes, ajoutent encore à son pouvoir de séduction. Il émane d'elle un étrange érotisme, sans doute alimenté par sa propre vie sentimentale à la fois tumultueuse et ambiguë. Dans les scènes d'amour, elle parvient toujours insensiblement à prendre le dessus.

Enfin, et surtout, Greta Garbo est une formidable actrice. Protégeant jalousement son secret, elle refuse de répéter les scènes et tourne à l'abri des regards et de toute perturbation extérieure, allant parfois jusqu'à chasser le réalisateur. Mais lorsqu'elle arrive sur le plateau, elle connaît son texte sur le bout des doigts et semble incapable de faire un faux pas. Sous ses dehors habituellement léthargiques, elle aborde son métier avec le plus grand sérieux et se montre inflexible quant aux conditions de tournage. Sans doute l'intransigeant Stiller lui a-t-il inculqué une discipline qui consiste à répéter méticuleusement son rôle pendant les longues heures qu'elle passe retranchée dans son univers secret, et qui, combinée à son instinct infaillible et à ses dons innés, engendre cette extraordinaire présence à l'écran.

OPPOSITE/RECHTS/CI-CONTRE
PORTRAIT
The last 50 years of her life were spent dodging photographers whenever she went out in public. / In den letzten 50 Jahren ihres Lebens ging sie bei jedem Schritt in der Öffentlichkeit den Fotoreportern aus dem Weg. / Pendant les 50 dernières années de sa vie, elle évitera les photographes à chaque sortie publique.

PAGE 22
PORTRAIT FOR 'GÖSTA BERLINGS SAGA'
('THE ATONEMENT OF GOSTA BERLING', 1924)

PAGES 24/25
STILL FROM 'LUFFAR-PETTER' ('PETER THE TRAMP', 1922)
Greta, Tyra Ryman and Iréne Zetterberg as Swedish bathing beauties. When it started to rain, Greta improvised a rain dance. / Greta Garbo, Tyra Ryman und Iréne Zetterberg als schwedische Badenixen: Als es zu regnen begann, improvisierte Greta einen Regentanz. / Greta, Tyra Ryman et Iréne Zetterberg en naïades suédoises.

2

VISUAL
FILMOGRAPHY

FILMOGRAFIE IN BILDERN
FILMOGRAPHIE EN IMAGES

EUROPE

EUROPA

EUROPE

STILL FROM 'GÖSTA BERLINGS SAGA' ('THE ATONEMENT OF GOSTA BERLING', 1924)
Director Mauritz Stiller gave Greta a role in this famous romantic saga. She was afraid because she had so little acting experience. / Der Regisseur Mauritz Stiller gab Greta eine Rolle in dieser berühmten romantischen Saga. Sie fürchtete allerdings, ihre Schauspielerfahrung reiche noch nicht aus. / Encore craintive et inexpérimentée, Greta décroche un rôle dans cette célèbre saga romantique grâce au réalisateur Mauritz Stiller.

PAGES 28/29
STILL FROM 'DIE FREUDLOSE GASSE' ('THE JOYLESS STREET', 1925)
Rechristened Greta Garbo by Stiller, she worked 12–14 hours a day on this German film, after which Stiller would coach her for the next day's work. / Unter dem Künstlernamen Greta Garbo, den ihr Stiller gegeben hatte, arbeitete sie täglich 12 bis 14 Stunden an diesem deutschen Film, und abends bereitete Stiller sie auf den nächsten Drehtag vor. / Pour le tournage de ce film allemand, Stiller, qui l'a rebaptisée Greta Garbo, la fait travailler 12 à 14 heures par jour avant de lui faire répéter les scènes du lendemain.

"When I make a picture I give everything of myself to it."
Greta Garbo

„Wenn ich einen Film drehe, dann gebe ich alles, was in mir steckt."
Greta Garbo

STILL FROM 'GÖSTA BERLINGS SAGA' ('THE ATONEMENT OF GOSTA BERLING', 1924)
Greta with Lars Hanson (as Gosta). The two-part film ran to almost four hours and got bad reviews locally, although it was a hit overseas. / Greta mit Lars Hanson (als Gösta). Der Zweiteiler hatte eine Spielzeit von fast vier Stunden. Der Film erntete in seinem Heimatland schlechte Kritiken, wurde allerdings im Ausland zum Kassenschlager. / Avec Lars Hanson (dans le rôle de Gösta). Mal accueilli par la critique suédoise, ce film en deux parties, long de près de quatre heures, fait un tabac à l'étranger.

« Quand je fais un film, je me donne entièrement. »
Greta Garbo

PAGE 30
PORTRAIT (6 JULY 1925)
Stiller and Garbo were given a contract by MGM in Hollywood. When Garbo arrived in New York she did not get a big studio welcome – the sympathetic photographer carried on taking photos even though he did not have film in his camera. / Stiller und Garbo wurden von MGM in Hollywood unter Vertrag genommen. Als Garbo in New York ankam, bereitete ihr das Studio keinen großen Empfang. Aus Mitleid mit ihr tat der Fotograf so, als würde er weitere Bilder von ihr schießen, obwohl er längst keinen Film mehr in der Kamera hatte. / Stiller et Garbo décrochent un contrat avec la MGM à Hollywood. À son arrivée à New York, voyant qu'elle n'est pas accueillie en fanfare, le photographe compatissant continue à la mitrailler bien qu'il n'ait plus de pellicule.

HOLLYWOOD

HOLLYWOOD

HOLLYWOOD

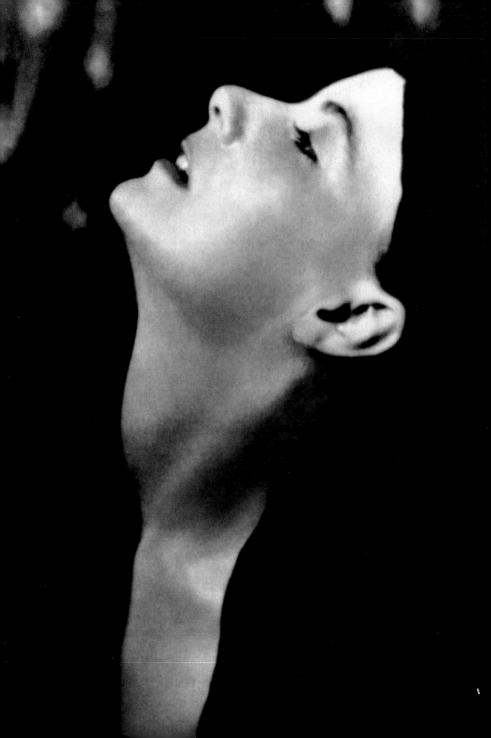

PORTRAIT (10 SEPTEMBER 1925)
Stiller and Garbo arrive in Los Angeles, welcomed by
the Swedish film community. / Bei ihrer Ankunft in Los
Angeles werden Stiller und Garbo von anderen
schwedischen Filmschaffenden begrüßt. / À leur
arrivée à Los Angeles, Stiller et Garbo sont accueillis
par la communauté suédoise.

PORTRAIT (1925)
Garbo spent two months in New York learning English
and having her portrait taken. This portrait by Arnold
Genthe appeared in 'Vanity Fair.' / Garbo blieb zwei
Monate in New York, um Englisch zu lernen und
Porträtaufnahmen zu machen. Diese Aufnahme von
Arnold Genthe erschien in *Vanity Fair*. / Garbo passe
deux mois à New York pour apprendre l'anglais et se
faire tirer le portrait, comme dans cette photo d'Arnold
Genthe publiée dans *Vanity Fair*.

"There are many things in your heart you can never tell another person. They are you, your private joys and sorrows, and you can never tell them. You cheapen yourself, the inside of yourself, when you tell them."
Greta Garbo

„Man trägt viel im Herzen, was man nie einem anderen Menschen mitteilen kann. Da steht man mit seinen privaten Freuden und Sorgen, und man kann nie darüber reden. Man wertet sich selbst ab, wenn man davon erzählt."
Greta Garbo

«On a beaucoup de choses au fond du cœur qu'on ne peut raconter à personne. Ce sont nos joies et nos peines secrètes, ce qui fait que nous sommes nous-mêmes. Ce serait indigne de raconter ce qu'on a au fond de soi.»
Greta Garbo

ON THE SET OF 'THE TORRENT' (1926)
Arriving on the noisy set of her first Hollywood film, Garbo was nervous and apprehensive. The studio appointed Sven-Hugo Borg as her interpreter so that she knew what everybody was saying. / Am lärmenden Set ihres ersten Hollywoodfilms war Garbo ängstlich und nervös. Das Studio stellte ihr Sven-Hugo Borg als Dolmetscher zur Seite, damit sie immer wusste, was die anderen sagten. / Pleine d'appréhension à son arrivée sur le plateau bruyant de son premier film hollywoodien, Garbo bénéficie des services d'un interprète, Sven-Hugo Borg, pour pouvoir suivre les conversations.

ON THE SET OF 'THE TORRENT' (1926)

As light was fading, director Monta Bell (right) filmed a bomb exploding but it didn't work and he needed a retake. When Sven-Hugo Borg went to fetch Garbo he found her extracting bomb fragments from her lips. She told Bell that he would have to wait. After all, there were plenty of other sunsets. / Im Licht der Dämmerung drehte Regisseur Monta Bell (rechts) die Explosion einer Bombe, doch der erste Versuch misslang. Als Sven-Hugo Borg Garbo für die Wiederholung zurückholen wollte, zog sie sich gerade die Bombensplitter aus den Lippen. Sie ließ Bell wissen, dass er sich gedulden müsse – schließlich gebe es noch genügend andere Sonnenuntergänge. / À la tombée du jour, le réalisateur Monta Bell (à droite) filme l'explosion d'une bombe. La scène étant ratée, il fait appeler Garbo pour une deuxième prise. L'actrice, qui est en train d'extraire des fragments de bombe de ses lèvres, lui demande d'attendre. Après tout, ce ne sont pas les couchers de soleil qui manquent.

"It's all a terrible compromise. There is no time for art. All that matters is what they call box office."
Greta Garbo

STILL FROM 'THE TORRENT' (1926)
Relations were not cordial between Garbo and her
leading man Ricardo Cortez. After filming the storm
sequence, Cortez took her blankets. She told Sven-
Hugo Borg not to let himself be bothered about a
"pumpkin" like that. / Das Verhältnis zwischen Garbo
und ihrem Filmpartner Ricardo Cortez war alles andere
als herzlich. Nach den Dreharbeiten für die Sturm-
sequenz nahm er ihr die Decken weg. Sven-Hugo Borg
sagte sie, er solle sich von einem „Kürbis" wie Cortez
nicht aus der Ruhe bringen lassen. / Les relations ne
sont guère cordiales entre Garbo et son partenaire,
Ricardo Cortez. Après la scène de l'orage, Cortez lui
confisque ses couvertures et elle conseille à Sven-Hugo
Borg de ne pas se laisser embêter par cette espèce de
« grande courge ».

„Es ist alles ein schrecklicher Kompromiss.
Für Kunst bleibt keine Zeit. Alles, was zählt, ist das,
was sie die ‚Kinokasse' nennen."
Greta Garbo

« C'est un perpétuel compromis. Il n'y a pas de
temps pour l'art. Tout ce qui compte, c'est ce qu'ils
appellent le box-office. »
Greta Garbo

STILL FROM 'THE TORRENT' (1926)
Ricardo Cortez was envious of the attention Garbo got
from the studio, and resented the fact that Garbo got
the role he wanted for his girlfriend, so he made life
miserable for her. In newsreel footage, he even stood
directly in front of her. / Ricardo Cortez beneidete
Garbo um die Aufmerksamkeit, die ihr seitens des
Studios zuteil wurde. Er nahm ihr übel, dass sie die Rolle
erhielt, in der er lieber seine Freundin gesehen hätte,
und machte ihr das Leben zur Hölle. In einer
Wochenschauaufnahme stellte er sich sogar genau vor
sie. / Jaloux des égards du studio pour Garbo, dont il
espérait le rôle pour sa petite amie, Ricardo Cortez lui
empoisonne la vie. Dans des images diffusées aux
actualités, on le voit se planter juste devant elle.

PORTRAIT FOR 'THE TORRENT' (1926)
Garbo plays a Spanish serving girl who becomes a
famous singer, while her true love, having rejected her
in deference to his family's wishes, lives a traditional
and unfulfilled life. / Garbo spielt ein spanisches
Dienstmädchen, das als Sängerin berühmt wird,
während das Leben ihres Geliebten, der unter dem
Druck seiner Familie die Beziehung beendet hat, in
traditionellen Bahnen verläuft und unerfüllt bleibt. /
Garbo incarne une servante espagnole qui devient une
chanteuse célèbre, tandis que l'homme qu'elle aime,
et qui l'a rejetée pour obéir à sa famille, mène une vie
conventionnelle et monotone.

PORTRAIT (1926)
Garbo lost faith in publicity departments after these
stunts and refused to do any further pictures for them. /
Nach diesen Mätzchen hatte Garbo genug von den
Publicityabteilungen und lehnte alle weiteren Aufnahmen ab. / Après ces séances de pose, Garbo
refusera de se plier aux lubies des publicitaires,
en qui elle a perdu toute confiance.

PORTRAIT (1926)
With the success of 'The Torrent' MGM made a lot of
silly publicity pictures of Garbo. / Nach dem Erfolg von
Fluten der Leidenschaft ließ MGM Garbo für eine
Vielzahl alberner Publicityfotos posieren. / Avec le
succès du *Torrent*, la MGM multiplie les photos
publicitaires les plus abracadabrantes.

PAGES 42/43
PORTRAIT (1926)
Garbo posed with lion cubs, but balked at posing with a
fully grown lion. She later maintained that this was a
trick photo. / Garbo posierte mit Löwenjungen, doch
mit einem ausgewachsenen Löwen traute sie sich nicht.
Später behauptete sie, dieses Foto sei eine Montage. /
Si elle accepte de poser avec des lionceaux, Garbo
rechigne à s'exposer en compagnie d'un lion adulte. Elle
prétendra par la suite qu'il s'agit d'une photo truquée.

ON THE SET OF 'THE TEMPTRESS' (1926)
Whilst filming this scene, Garbo received news of her
sister's death. She said that filming must continue. / Bei
den Aufnahmen zu dieser Szene erfuhr Garbo vom Tod
ihrer Schwester. Sie bestand darauf, die Dreharbeiten
fortzusetzen. / Garbo, qui apprend la mort de sa sœur
pendant le tournage de cette scène, insiste pour
poursuivre le travail.

PAGES 46/47
ON THE SET OF 'THE TEMPTRESS' (1926)
When filming began on 26 March 1926, Stiller (left)
found work difficult because he had not learned English
or adapted to American methods of production. / Die
Dreharbeiten, die am 26. März 1926 begannen, waren
für Stiller (links) anstrengend, weil er weder Englisch
gelernt, noch sich den amerikanischen Produktions-
methoden angepasst hatte. / Lorsque débute le
tournage, le 26 mars 1926, Stiller (à gauche) souffre d'un
double handicap : il n'a pas appris l'anglais et ne s'est pas
adapté aux méthodes de production américaines.

ON THE SET OF 'THE TEMPTRESS' (1926)
To prepare for her new film with Mauritz Stiller, Garbo
learned how to ride a horse and fall from it without
hurting herself. / Zur Vorbereitung ihres neuen Films
mit Mauritz Stiller lernte Garbo zu reiten und vom Pferd
zu fallen, ohne sich zu verletzen. / Pour préparer son
nouveau film avec Mauritz Stiller, Garbo apprend à
monter à cheval et à tomber sans se blesser.

ON THE SET OF 'THE TEMPTRESS' (1926)

MGM fired Stiller (left) because he was too slow and expensive. They replaced him with Fred Niblo, who had saved 'Ben-Hur.' / MGM feuerte Stiller (links), weil er dem Studio zu langsam und zu teuer war. Man ersetzte ihn durch Fred Niblo, der bereits zuvor *Ben Hur* gerettet hatte. / Jugé trop lent et trop cher, Stiller (à gauche) est renvoyé par la MGM. Il est remplacé par Fred Niblo, qui a sauvé *Ben-Hur*.

PAGES 50/51

STILL FROM 'THE TEMPTRESS' (1926)

Antonio Moreno plays an engineer building a dam in South America. He is pursued by Garbo. All the men, including the local bandits, desire her. / Antonio Moreno spielt einen Ingenieur, der in Südamerika einen Staudamm baut. Er wird von Elena (Garbo) verfolgt, die von allen Männern begehrt wird. / Antonio Moreno incarne un ingénieur chargé de construire un barrage en Amérique du Sud. Garbo, qui le suit à la trace, est convoitée par toute la gent masculine, y compris les bandits.

STILL FROM 'THE TEMPTRESS' (1926)

Garbo plays a vamp – a woman whose presence drives men (in this case Antonio Moreno) mad with desire. / Garbo spielt einen Vamp – eine Frau, die allein durch ihre Anwesenheit Männer (hier Antonio Moreno) vor Lust in den Wahnsinn treibt. / Garbo incarne une femme fatale dont la présence rend les hommes (en l'occurrence, Antonio Moreno) fous de désir.

STILL FROM 'THE TEMPTRESS' (1926)
The lovers first meet at a party and have a magical night
together. / Die Liebenden lernen sich auf einer Party
kennen und verbringen eine wunderbare Nacht
miteinander. / Les deux amants se rencontrent à une
fête et passent ensemble une nuit de rêve.

STILL FROM 'THE TEMPTRESS' (1926)
At the end of the film, Moreno is blinded by the bandit
during a duel. Garbo leaves Moreno so that he can
complete the dam. / Gegen Ende des Films verliert
Manuel (Moreno) beim Duell mit einem Banditen sein
Augenlicht. Elena (Garbo) verlässt ihn, damit er den
Damm fertig stellen kann. / À la fin du film, Moreno
perd la vue lors d'un duel avec un bandit. Garbo le
quitte pour qu'il puisse achever le barrage.

"She can 'feel' light."
Clarence Sinclair Bull, portrait photographer

„*Sie kann das Licht ,spüren'.*"
Clarence Sinclair Bull, Porträtfotograf

« *Elle 'sent' la lumière.* »
Clarence Sinclair Bull, photographe portraitiste

STILL FROM 'FLESH AND THE DEVIL' (1927)
MGM wanted Garbo to start on a new film, but she
wanted time to mourn her sister and she certainly did
not want to play another vamp. MGM reacted by
arranging unfavourable press in the newspapers and
Garbo relented. She had an instant rapport with her
costar John Gilbert and they became lovers. / MGM
wollte, dass Garbo mit dem Dreh zu einem neuen Film
begann, doch sie wollte sich Zeit für die Trauer um ihre
Schwester nehmen. Außerdem wollte sie auf keinen Fall
wieder einen Vamp spielen. MGM lancierte einige
negative Schlagzeilen, und sie gab nach. Mit ihrem
Filmpartner John Gilbert verstand sie sich auf Anhieb,
und die beiden wurden auch privat ein Liebespaar. /
Alors que Garbo refuse d'enchaîner avec un nouveau
rôle de femme fatale après la mort de sa sœur, la MGM
parvient à la faire céder en montant la presse contre
elle. Le courant passe immédiatement avec son
partenaire John Gilbert, dont elle devient la maîtresse.

STILL FROM 'FLESH AND THE DEVIL' (1927)
John Gilbert begins an affair with Garbo unaware that
she is married. When they are discovered, Gilbert must
fight a duel with her husband. / Als Leo van Harden
(John Gilbert) eine Affäre mit Felicitas (Garbo) beginnt,
weiß er nicht, dass sie verheiratet ist. Als das Paar
entdeckt wird, muss sich Leo mit ihrem Ehemann
duellieren. / Dans le film, John Gilbert devient l'amant
de Garbo, ignorant qu'elle est mariée. Surpris par son
époux, il doit se battre en duel.

*"She must never create situations. She must be
thrust into them. The drama comes in how she
rides them out."*
Irving Thalberg, MGM Executive

STILL FROM 'FLESH AND THE DEVIL' (1927)
Having killed Garbo's husband in a duel, Gilbert must go
away for some time. The lovers promise to be faithful. /
Nachdem er den Ehemann seiner Geliebten im Duell
getötet hat, muss Leo (Gilbert) für einige Zeit
verschwinden. Die Liebenden geloben, einander treu zu
bleiben. / Après avoir tué le mari en duel, Gilbert doit
s'exiler quelque temps. Les amants font serment de
fidélité.

*„Sie darf keine Situationen erschaffen. Sie muss in
sie hineingeworfen werden. Das Drama entsteht
durch ihre Art der Bewältigung."*
Irving Thalberg, Produzent bei MGM

*« Il ne faut pas lui demander de créer les
situations. Il faut la jeter dedans. Le ressort
dramatique découle de la façon dont elle les
surmonte. »*
Irving Thalberg, producteur de la MGM

"I don't think she is conscious of movement, voice, or expression. She just seems to think her part, and everything about it expresses it to perfection. That is why we use so many close-ups. She can tell so much with the subtlest glance of an eye and put so much meaning into a fleeting expression. In a more distant shot those subtleties would be lost."
William Daniels, cinematographer

„Ich glaube nicht, dass sie sich ihrer Bewegungen, ihrer Stimme oder ihres Ausdrucks bewusst ist. Sie scheint sich nur in ihre Rolle hineinzudenken, und dann drückt alles an ihr diese Rolle in Vollendung aus. Deshalb machen wir ja so viele Nahaufnahmen. Sie kann mit dem kleinsten Augenaufschlag so viel sagen und so viel Bedeutung in einen flüchtigen Ausdruck hineinlegen. Diese Feinheiten gingen in einer Totale verloren."
William Daniels, Kameramann

« Je ne crois pas qu'elle soit consciente de ses mouvements, de ses inflexions de voix ni de ses expressions. Elle semble seulement intérioriser son rôle et l'exprimer en tous points à la perfection. C'est pourquoi nous faisons autant de gros plans. Elle peut exprimer tant de choses avec un subtil coup d'œil ou une expression fugitive. Dans des plans plus éloignés, ces subtilités passeraient inaperçues. »
William Daniels, chef opérateur

ON THE SET OF 'FLESH AND THE DEVIL' (1927)
Gilbert entrusts Garbo to his best friend Lars Hanson, who then marries her. Clarence Brown (above Garbo) directed her six times, whilst she worked with cinematographer William Daniels (above the camera) on 21 films. / Leo (Gilbert) vertraut Felicitas (Garbo) seinem besten Freund Ulrich (Lars Hanson) an, der sie schließlich heiratet. Garbo spielte sechsmal unter der Regie von Clarence Brown (im Bild hinter ihr), während sie in 21 Filmen mit Kameramann William Daniels (oberhalb der Kamera) arbeitete. / Le héros confie sa maîtresse à son meilleur ami (Lars Hanson), qui finit par l'épouser. Garbo tournera six fois sous la direction de Clarence Brown (derrière elle) et 21 fois avec le chef opérateur William Daniels (au-dessus de la caméra).

PAGES 60/61
STILL FROM 'FLESH AND THE DEVIL' (1927)
When Gilbert returns from exile, he tries to kill Garbo rather than let her destroy his best friend. / Als Leo (Gilbert) aus seinem Exil zurückkehrt, versucht er, Felicitas (Garbo) zu töten, bevor sie seinen besten Freund ins Verderben stürzt. / Lorsque le héros rentre d'exil, il préfère tenter de tuer son ancienne maîtresse plutôt que de la laisser détruire son meilleur ami.

ON THE SET OF 'FLESH AND THE DEVIL' (1927)
The love affair was obvious for all to see, although it often erupted in arguments concerning Gilbert's excessive drinking. / Ihre Liebesbeziehung war für alle offensichtlich, obwohl es häufig Streit gab, weil Gilbert zu viel trank. / La liaison entre les deux acteurs saute aux yeux, même si le penchant de Gilbert pour l'alcool donne souvent lieu à des disputes.

"I didn't want to know the people I was acting with. I couldn't go out to dinner with my leading man and hear about his wife and family. I just wanted to meet [them] as strangers on a set."
Greta Garbo

„Ich wollte die Leute, mit denen ich vor der Kamera stand, nicht kennen lernen. Ich hätte unmöglich mit meinem Filmpartner zum Abendessen ausgehen und mir dann Geschichten von seiner Frau und seinen Kindern anhören können. Ich wollte [sie] einfach nur als Fremde am Set treffen."
Greta Garbo

STILL FROM 'A MAN'S MAN' (1929)
Garbo and Gilbert had a cameo appearance arriving at
a film premiere. It was an in-joke, because Garbo usually
avoided premieres – she preferred going to cinemas
incognito and sitting with an audience. / Garbo und
Gilbert erschienen unangemeldet zur Uraufführung des
Films. Der Auftritt kam überraschend, weil Garbo nie
Filmpremieren besuchte, sondern lieber inkognito ins
Kino ging und sich unters Publikum mischte. / Garbo et
Gilbert apparaissent brièvement à la première d'un film,
clin d'œil au fait que l'actrice boude généralement les
premières, préférant se mêler incognito au public d'une
salle de cinéma.

« Je ne souhaitais pas connaître les acteurs avec
qui je jouais. Je ne pouvais pas aller dîner avec
mon partenaire et l'entendre parler de sa femme
et de ses enfants. Je voulais qu'ils soient des
étrangers sur le plateau. »
Greta Garbo

ON THE SET OF 'LOVE' (1927)

MGM offered Garbo bad projects: when she refused, the company suspended her without pay in a ploy to persuade her to sign a longer contract at the same rate of pay. She called their bluff, got a better contract and began work with director Dimitri Buchowetzki (in front of camera). / MGM bot Garbo miese Rollen an, die sie ablehnte. Dafür wurde sie von MGM unbezahlt beurlaubt. So wollte MGM sie zwingen, einen längeren Vertrag – ohne eine Erhöhung ihrer Gage – zu unterschreiben. Sie ließ sich jedoch nicht bluffen, erhielt sogar bessere Konditionen und begann die Arbeit mit Regisseur Dimitri Buchowetzki (vor der Kamera). / Lorsque Garbo refuse les mauvais films qu'on lui propose, la MGM la suspend sans rémunération, afin de lui imposer ses conditions. Garbo tient bon, obtient une augmentation et entame le tournage avec le réalisateur Dimitri Buchowetzki (devant la caméra).

"Certain great actors possess what seems to be an uncanny ability to register thought. Lon Chaney was one. Garbo is another ... Garbo is more sensitive to emotion than film is to light."
Victor Sjöström

„Manche großen Schauspieler besitzen eine unheimliche Fähigkeit, Gedanken zu lesen. Lon Chaney war einer von ihnen und Garbo eine andere ... Greta Garbo reagiert auf Gefühle empfindlicher als Film auf Licht."
Victor Sjöström

« Certains grands acteurs semblent posséder une étrange capacité à exprimer la pensée. C'était le cas de Lon Chaney. C'est aussi celui de Garbo ... Garbo est plus sensible aux émotions que la pellicule à la lumière. »
Victor Sjöström

STILL FROM 'LOVE' (1927)
Leading man Ricardo Cortez was more respectful than he had been on 'The Torrent'. Even so, the direction was bad and Garbo's five-week illness gave studio head Irving Thalberg an opportunity to scrap the film. / Ihr Filmpartner Ricardo Cortez erwies ihr diesmal etwas mehr Respekt als bei den Dreharbeiten zu *Fluten der Leidenschaft*. Allerdings war die Regie schwach, und Garbos fünfwöchige Erkrankung gab Studioboss Irving Thalberg die willkommene Gelegenheit, das Projekt zu stoppen. / Son partenaire Ricardo Cortez se montre plus respectueux que sur le tournage du *Torrent*. Mais la réalisation est déplorable et les cinq semaines de maladie de Garbo donnent au producteur Irving Thalberg un prétexte pour mettre le film au placard.

PORTRAIT FOR 'LOVE' (1927)
With Edmund Goulding as director, and John Gilbert cast as Alexei Vronsky, the production of this adaptation of Tolstoy's *Anna Karenina* started again with real chemistry. / Unter dem neuen Regisseur Edmund Goulding und mit John Gilbert in der Rolle des Alexej Wronskij begann die Produktion dieser Adaption von Tolstois *Anna Karenina* erneut - und diesmal stimmte die Chemie. / Avec Edmund Goulding à la réalisation et John Gilbert dans le rôle d'Alexei Vronsky dans cette adaptation d'*Anna Karénine*, le tournage reprend et le courant passe.

ON THE SET OF 'LOVE' (1927)
Unusually, Garbo allowed informal photos like this one to be taken on the set. The relaxed production finished filming after only 28 days. / Spontane Fotos wie dieses während der Dreharbeiten, die diesmal ganz entspannt nach nur 28 Tagen zu Ende gingen, gestattete Greta Garbo sonst nicht. / Il est rare que Garbo se laisse ainsi prendre en photo à l'improviste sur le plateau. L'atmosphère détendue permet de boucler le tournage en 28 jours seulement.

STILL FROM 'LOVE' (1927)
Tolstoy's classic novel follows Anna's journey as she
gives up her son (Brandon Hurst) to live outside society
with her lover. In the end, she finds out that it was all for
nothing. / Tolstois Romanklassiker folgt dem Schicksal
Annas, die ihren Sohn (Brandon Hurst) aufgibt, um mit
ihrem Liebhaber ein Leben fernab gesellschaftlicher
Koventionen zu beginnen. Am Ende findet sie heraus,
dass all ihre Opfer umsonst waren. / Le roman de
Tolstoï suit les aventures d'Anna, qui abandonne son fils
(Brandon Hurst) pour vivre en marge de la société avec
son amant. Mais ce sacrifice sera vain.

ADVERT FOR 'LOVE' (1927)
MGM employed innovative advertising techniques to
sell Garbo's films to the cinema trade. / MGM bediente
sich innovativer Werbestrategien, um den Kinobesitzern
Garbos Film schmackhaft zu machen. / La MGM
emploie des méthodes publicitaires innovantes pour
vendre les films de Garbo aux distributeurs.

THE GIRL FRIEND KNOWS HER ONIONS!

She only has to mention that tonight's show is John Gilbert and Greta Garbo in "Love"—and blooie goes the bridge game!

it's cold outside!

it's steam-heated indoors!

YOU'VE got to have **STRONG** attractions **TO** drag them out of **COZY** homes these nights! **IT'S** smart business to

STILL FROM 'THE DIVINE WOMAN' (1928)
Only one scene still exists of this lost film, directed by
Victor Sjöström and costarring Lars Hanson as the
loving husband who gives up his army career for her. /
Von diesem verschollenen Film existiert nur noch eine
einzige Szene. Regie führte Victor Sjöström, und Lars
Hanson spielte den liebevollen Ehemann, der für
Marianne seine Karriere beim Heer aufgibt. / Il ne
subsiste qu'une seule scène de ce film réalisé par Victor
Sjöström, avec Lars Hanson dans le rôle du mari qui
abandonne sa carrière militaire par amour pour Garbo.

STILL FROM 'THE DIVINE WOMAN' (1928)
Marianne (Garbo) becomes a theatre star after her
husband is jailed. / Nachdem ihr Mann im Gefängnis
gelandet ist, wird Marianne (Garbo) zum Bühnenstar. /
Une fois son mari en prison, l'héroïne devient une
vedette du théâtre.

STILL FROM 'THE MYSTERIOUS LADY' (1928)
Garbo romances Conrad Nagel who is unaware that she
is a spy. / Tanja (Garbo) umgarnt Hauptmann von Raden
(Conrad Nagel), der nicht ahnt, dass sie eine Spionin
ist. / Garbo séduit Conrad Nagel, qui ignore qu'elle est
une espionne.

PAGES 74/75
**ON THE SET OF 'THE MYSTERIOUS LADY'
(1928)**
Musicians create the mood for the actors as William
Daniels and director Fred Niblo ride with the camera. /
Musiker bringen die Schauspieler in Stimmung, während
Kameramann William Daniels und Regisseur Fred Niblo
mit der Kamera fahren. / Des musiciens interprètent
une musique d'ambiance, tandis que William Daniels et
le réalisateur Fred Niblo suivent la caméra.

STILL FROM 'THE MYSTERIOUS LADY' (1928)
Like other foreign stars, Garbo brought a new eroticism
to the cinema. She created a sensation in 'Flesh and
the Devil' with her open-mouth and reclining kisses.
She made sex seem totally natural. / Wie viele andere
ausländische Stars, brachte auch Greta Garbo eine
neue Erotik auf die Leinwand. Ihre Küsse mit geöffne-
tem Mund und zurückgelehntem Kopf in *Es war* sorgten
seinerzeit für großes Aufsehen. Sex schien bei ihr die
natürlichste Sache der Welt. / Comme beaucoup de
stars étrangères, Garbo apporte une nouvelle forme
d'érotisme au cinéma. Dans *La Chair et le Diable*, elle
fait sensation avec ses baisers torrides. Chez elle, le
sexe semble la chose la plus naturelle du monde.

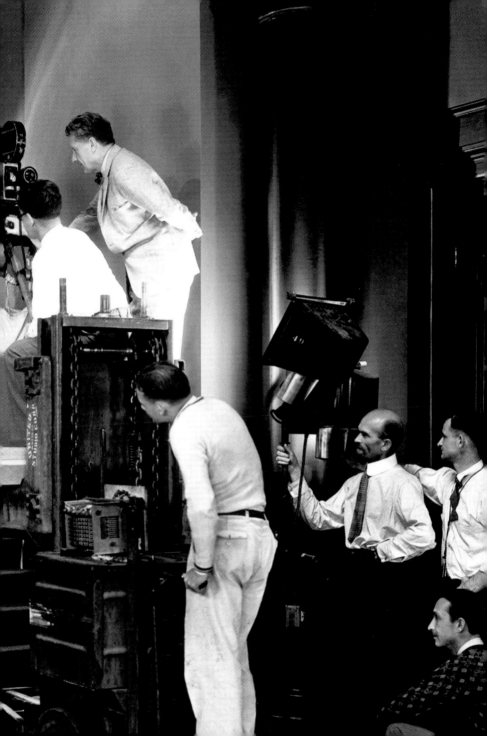

STILL FROM 'A WOMAN OF AFFAIRS' (1928)
After a miscarriage, Garbo grasps roses as if cradling
her unborn child before going to join her lover John
Gilbert. Many critics consider it her finest scene in a
silent film. / Nach einer Fehlgeburt wiegt Diana (Garbo)
einen Strauß Rosen so zärtlich wie ihr verlorenes Kind
in den Armen und geht anschließend zu ihrem
Liebhaber (John Gilbert). Viele Kritiker halten diese
Szene für die beste in all ihren Stummfilmen. / Après
une fausse couche, l'héroïne étreint un bouquet de
roses comme pour bercer l'enfant disparu, puis va
retrouver son amant (John Gilbert). De nombreux
critiques considèrent cette scène comme la meilleure
de ses films muets.

*"Why should this strange sort of beauty affect
millions more deeply than some bright and
sparkling pin-up girl?"*
Béla Balázs, writer

*„Warum beeinflusste diese merkwürdige Art
von Schönheit Millionen stärker als irgendein
strahlendes und funkelndes Pin-up-Girl?"*
Béla Balázs, Schriftsteller

*« Pourquoi cette étrange beauté toucherait-elle
plus profondément des millions de gens qu'une
éblouissante pin-up ? »*
Béla Balázs, écrivain

STILL FROM 'A WOMAN OF AFFAIRS' (1928)
Based on Michael Arlen's 'The Green Hat,' which is
about the shame and degradation of syphilis, the
subject matter was changed to embezzlement, so that
the film did not breach the Production Code. / Damit
die Selbstzensur den Film genehmigte, handelt er von
einer Unterschlagung und nicht, wie Michael Arlens
Romanvorlage *Der grüne Hut*, von der Schande und
Demütigung eines Syphiliskranken. / Inspiré du
Chapeau vert de Michael Arlen, qui évoque la
déchéance due à la syphilis, ce film opte pour un sujet
moins sulfureux, les détournements de fonds, afin
d'échapper à la censure.

PAGES 78/79
ON THE SET OF 'A WOMAN OF AFFAIRS' (1928)
Garbo observed that American directors concentrated
on the external aspects of a character, whereas Mauritz
Stiller taught her to work on the internal characteristics.
Cinematographer William Daniels (right) captured the
emotional energy she radiated during filming. / Garbo
beobachtete, dass sich amerikanische Regisseure eher
auf die äußerlichen Aspekte der Figuren konzentrierten,
während ihr Mauritz Stiller beigebracht hatte, sich mit
deren Innenleben auseinanderzusetzen. Kameramann
William Daniels (rechts) hielt die emotionale Energie im
Bild fest, die sie bei den Dreharbeiten ausstrahlte. /
Garbo remarque que les réalisateurs américains
se concentrent sur les aspects extérieurs des
personnages, alors que Mauritz Stiller lui a appris à
étudier leur richesse intérieure. Le chef opérateur
William Daniels (à droite) restitue la puissance
émotionnelle qui émane d'elle durant le tournage.

STILL FROM 'WILD ORCHIDS' (1929)
Nils Asther plays a sadistic Javanese prince who preys
upon Garbo. / Nils Asther spielt einen sadistischen
javanischen Prinzen, dem Lillie (Garbo) zum Opfer
fällt. / Nils Asther incarne un prince javanais sadique
qui tente de séduire Garbo.

"She hated the hypocrisy that was evident
all around her."
Frances Marion, screenwriter

„Sie hasste die Heuchelei, die überall in ihrem
Umfeld offensichtlich war."
Frances Marion, Drehbuchautorin

« Elle détestait l'hypocrisie qui se manifestait tout
autour d'elle. »
Frances Marion, scénariste

ON THE SET OF 'WILD ORCHIDS' (1929)
Whilst filming Garbo received news that Mauritz Stiller
had died in Stockholm. She was not allowed time off to
attend his funeral. / Während der Dreharbeiten erfuhr
Garbo, dass Mauritz Stiller in Stockholm gestorben war.
Sie erhielt aber keinen Urlaub von den Dreharbeiten für
einen Kondolenzbesuch. / Pendant le tournage, Garbo
apprend la mort de Mauritz Stiller à Stockholm, mais on
ne l'autorise pas à s'absenter pour lui rendre hommage.

PAGES 82/83
ON THE SET OF 'WILD ORCHIDS' (1929)
This lavish set shows the attention to detail that MGM
paid to their films. Garbo is seated at the front of the
set with Nils Asther and on-screen husband Lewis
Stone. The camera is in a 'basket' hung from the studio
ceiling, which allows it to 'fly' through the set. / Die
üppige Ausstattung zeigt, welch großen Wert MGM auf
Details legte. Garbo sitzt im Bild vorn mit Nils Asther
und Lewis Stone, der im Film ihren Ehemann spielt. Die
Kamera hängt in einem Korb von der Studiodecke und
kann auf diese Weise durch die Kulissen „fliegen". / Ce
luxueux décor montre le soin que la MGM apporte aux
détails. Garbo est assise à l'avant du plateau avec Nils
Asther et son mari (Lewis Stone). La caméra est dans un
« panier » suspendu au plafond afin de pouvoir survoler
le plateau.

STILL FROM 'WILD ORCHIDS' (1929)
The script was originally entitled 'Heat,' but MGM eventually realised that the tagline 'Greta Garbo in Heat' would not be acceptable for theatre advertising. / Das Drehbuch trug ursprünglich den Titel „Heat" („Hitze"), bis MGM bemerkte, dass der Werbeslogan „Greta Garbo in Heat" („Greta Garbo brünstig") auf den Kinoplakaten zu Missverständnissen führen könnte. / Le scénario est à l'origine intitulé « Heat », mais la MGM estime que le slogan « Greta Garbo in Heat » (Greta Garbo en « chaleur ») est un peu malvenu.

STILL FROM 'WILD ORCHIDS' (1929)
Garbo often expressed a wish to wear more masculine clothing on screen. / Garbo wünschte sich für ihre Filmrollen oft männlichere Kleidung. / Garbo exprime souvent le désir de porter des vêtements plus masculins à l'écran.

PAGES 86/87
STILL FROM 'THE SINGLE STANDARD' (1929)
The film asks whether or not there can be a single standard of behaviour for both men and women. / Der Film wirft die Frage auf, ob es für Männer und Frauen einheitliche Verhaltensregeln geben kann oder nicht. / La question soulevée par ce film est de savoir si le comportement des hommes et des femmes peut obéir aux mêmes normes.

STILL FROM 'THE SINGLE STANDARD' (1929)
For the first time, Garbo plays an attractive American woman whose life and desires were readily understandable to the big audience. / Zum ersten Mal spielt Garbo eine attraktive Amerikanerin, deren Leben und Sehnsüchte für die breite Masse nachvollziehbar sind. / Garbo interprète pour la première fois une belle Américaine dont la vie et les désirs sont à la portée de tous.

"Everything is built on movement. Garbo is all movement. First she gets the emotion, and out of the emotion comes the movement, and out of the movement comes the dialogue. She's so perfect that people say she can't act."
Louise Brooks

„Alles basiert auf Bewegung. Garbo ist ganz und gar Bewegung. Zuerst erfasst sie das Gefühl, und aus dem Gefühl erwächst die Bewegung, und aus der Bewegung der Dialog. Sie ist so perfekt, dass die Leute sagen, sie könne nicht schauspielern."
Louise Brooks

STILL FROM 'THE SINGLE STANDARD' (1929)
The relaxed attitude hides the fact that Garbo was
heartbroken over the marriage of John Gilbert to Ina
Claire. / Die entspannte Haltung täuscht darüber
hinweg, dass Garbo zu diesem Zeitpunkt untröstlich
war, weil John Gilbert Ina Claire geheiratet hatte. /
Malgré son air détendu, Garbo a le cœur brisé après le
mariage de John Gilbert avec Ina Claire.

« Tout est construit sur le mouvement. Garbo n'est
que mouvement. Elle ressent d'abord l'émotion,
puis de l'émotion jaillit le mouvement, et du
mouvement émane le dialogue. Elle est tellement
parfaite que les gens disent qu'elle ne sait pas
jouer. »
Louise Brooks

PAGES 90/91
STILL FROM 'THE SINGLE STANDARD' (1929)
Garbo proves that she can play a wife and mother just
as well as a mysterious vamp. / Garbo beweist, dass sie
eine Ehefrau und Mutter genauso gut spielen kann wie
den geheimnisumwitterten Vamp. / Garbo prouve
qu'elle peut aussi bien incarner une mère de famille
qu'une mystérieuse femme fatale.

"At 9 o'clock am the work may begin. 'Tell Miss Garbo we're ready,' says the director. 'I'm here,' a low voice answers, and she appears, perfectly dressed and combed as the scene needs. [...] And at 6 o'clock pm [...] she points at the watch and goes away giving you a sorry smile. She's very strict with herself [...]. She never looks at rushes nor goes to the premieres but some days later, early in the afternoon, enters all alone an outskirts movie house, [...] and gets out only when the projection finishes, masked with her sunglasses."

Jacques Feyder

„Nehmen wir an, die Arbeit beginnt um 9 Uhr. Der Regisseur sagt: ‚Sagen Sie Fräulein Garbo, dass wir bereit sind.‘ Da kommt die Antwort mit leiser Stimme: ‚Hier bin ich‘, und dann erscheint sie, tadellos gekleidet und frisiert, genau wie es die Szene erfordert. [...] Und um 18 Uhr [...] deutet sie auf die Uhr und verschwindet mit einem entschuldigenden Lächeln. Sie ist sehr streng mit sich selbst [...]. Sie schaut sich nie die Bildmuster an oder wohnt den Premieren bei, aber ein paar Tage danach geht sie am frühen Nachmittag irgendwo in der Vorstadt in ein Kino [...] und verlässt den Saal erst, wenn die Vorführung vorüber ist, maskiert mit ihrer Sonnenbrille.“

Jacques Feyder

«À 9 heures du matin, le travail peut commencer. ‚Dites à Mademoiselle Garbo que nous sommes prêts‘, annonce le réalisateur. ‚Je suis là‘, répond une voix sourde, et elle apparaît, parfaitement vêtue et coiffée comme l'exige la scène. [...] À 6 heures du soir, [...] elle indique l'horloge et s'en va avec un sourire désolé. Mais elle est très stricte avec elle-même [...]. Elle ne visionne jamais les rushes et n'assiste pas aux premières, mais quelques jours plus tard, en début d'après-midi, elle entre seule dans un cinéma de banlieue [...] et n'en ressort qu'à la fin de la projection, masquée par ses lunettes de soleil.»

Jacques Feyder

STILL FROM 'THE KISS' (1929)

Lew Ayres' first scene in the film was his kiss with Garbo. Afterwards, Garbo asked to be introduced to him - nobody had thought to do so in the rush to start filming. / Die erste Szene, die Lew Ayres für den Film drehte, war sein Kuss mit Garbo. Danach bat Garbo, ihm vorgestellt zu werden - was man in der Hektik des Drehbeginns völlig vergessen hatte. / Après avoir tourné avec Lew Ayres la scène du baiser, la première où il apparaît dans le film, Garbo demande à ce qu'on les présente, ce que personne n'a songé à faire dans la précipitation du tournage.

STILL FROM 'THE KISS' (1929)
Garbo shoots her husband, who had seen her kissing
the young man played by Lew Ayres. / Irene (Garbo)
erschießt ihren Ehemann, nachdem er sie und Pierre
(Lew Ayres) beim Küssen überrascht hat. / Garbo tire
sur son mari, qui l'a surprise en train d'embrasser Lew
Ayres.

PAGE 96
ON THE SET OF 'ANNA CHRISTIE' (1930)
Garbo and director Clarence Brown. 'Garbo Talks!'
announced the adverts. Her first words on film:
"Gimme a whiskey – ginger ale on the side." / Garbo und
Regisseur Clarence Brown. „Die Garbo spricht!"
verkündete die Werbung. Ihre ersten Worte auf der
Leinwand waren: „Gib mir einen Whiskey – und dazu ein
Ginger Ale." / En compagnie du réalisateur Clarence
Brown. « Garbo parle ! », clame la publicité. Ses premiers
mots à l'écran sont : « Donnez-moi un whisky et un
soda ».

ON THE SET OF 'THE KISS' (1929)
Director Jacques Feyder supervises Garbo being
defended in court by her lover Conrad Nagel. /
Regisseur Jacques Feyder berät Garbo während der
Prozessszene, in der Irene von ihrem Liebhaber André
(Conrad Nagel) verteidigt wird. / Garbo est défendue
au tribunal par son amant, Conrad Nagel, sous le regard
du réalisateur Jacques Feyder.

TALKIES

TONFILME

LES FILMS PARLANTS

STILL FROM 'ANNA CHRISTIE' (1930)
Garbo with experienced comic actress Marie Dressler,
who had fallen on hard times since starring with Charlie
Chaplin in 'Tillie's Punctured Romance.' / Garbo mit der
erfahrenen Komödiantin Marie Dressler, die seit ihrer
Rolle an der Seite Charlie Chaplins in *Tillies große
Romanze* persönlich schwere Zeiten durchgemacht
hatte. / Garbo en compagnie de l'actrice comique Marie
Dressler, qui a connu des années de vache maigre
depuis *Le Roman comique de Charlot et Lolotte* de
Chaplin.

STILL FROM 'ANNA CHRISTIE' (1930)
Garbo makes her entrance 15 minutes into this film
version of Eugene O'Neill's play. It was the top-grossing
film of 1930, earning $1.5 million worldwide. / In dieser
Verfilmung des Theaterstücks von Eugene O'Neill tritt
Garbo erstmals eine Viertelstunde nach Filmbeginn auf.
Weltweit spielte der Film, der 1930 der kommerziell
erfolgreichste Film war, 1,5 Millionen US-Dollar ein. /
Dans cette adaptation de la pièce d'Eugene O'Neill,
Garbo fait son entrée au bout de 15 minutes. Avec 1,5
million de dollars de recettes, ce film est le plus gros
succès commercial de 1930.

STILL FROM 'ANNA CHRISTIE' (1930)
Garbo is a fallen woman who stays on her father's barge
out of necessity. When she meets rough and ready
Irishman Charles Bickford, she is tempted back to her
loose ways. / Garbo spielt ein gefallenes Mädchen, das
aus Not auf dem Kahn ihres Vaters bleibt. Als sie den
ungeschlachten Iren Matt Burke (Charles Bickford)
kennen lernt, ist sie versucht, wieder in ihren
liederlichen Lebenswandel zurückzufallen. / Garbo
incarne une femme déchue qui en est réduite à vivre
sur la péniche de son père. Lorsqu'elle rencontre un
rude Irlandais (Charles Bickford), elle est tentée de
retomber dans la débauche.

*"She is a great artist, but it is both her supreme
glory and her supreme tragedy that art is to her
the only reality … It is only when she breathes the
breath of life into a part, clothes with her own flesh
and blood the concept of the playwright that she
herself is fully awake, fully alive."*
Marie Dressler

*„Sie ist eine große Künstlerin, aber es ist sowohl
die Grundlage ihres Ruhmes als auch ihre äußerste
Tragik, dass die Kunst ihre einzige Wirklichkeit ist …
Nur wenn sie einer Rolle Leben einhaucht, den
Entwurf eines Dramatikers mit ihrem eigenen
Fleisch und Blut erfüllt, ist sie selbst vollkommen
wach, vollkommen lebendig."*
Marie Dressler

STILL FROM 'ANNA CHRISTIE' (1930)
The daughter wants to live up to the ideals of her father (here played by George F. Marion, who starred in the original Broadway play) but at the same time she needs freedom to live her own life. / Die Tochter würde gerne den Idealen ihres Vaters (George F. Marion, der die Rolle bereits am Broadway spielte) gerecht werden, doch braucht sie auch Freiräume, um ihr eigenes Leben zu leben. / Soucieuse d'être à la hauteur des idéaux de son père (George F. Marion, qui interprétait déjà ce rôle dans la pièce à Broadway), elle a également besoin de vivre sa propre vie.

« C'est une grande artiste, mais sa gloire suprême et sa suprême tragédie est que l'art constitue pour elle la seule réalité ... Elle ne se sent pleinement éveillée et pleinement en vie que quand elle insuffle elle-même la vie à un personnage et habille de sa chair et de son sang le concept imaginé par l'auteur. »
Marie Dressler

STILL FROM 'ANNA CHRISTIE' (GERMAN VERSION, 1930)
MGM experimented by making a German-language version of the film with German actors to avoid bad dubbing and translations of their film. Luckily, Garbo spoke German. / MGM experimentierte damit, auch eine deutsche Fassung des Films mit deutschen Schauspielern zu drehen, um eine schlechte Übersetzung und Synchronisation zu vermeiden. Zum Glück sprach Garbo Deutsch. / Afin d'éviter les problèmes de traduction et de doublage, la MGM décide de tourner une version allemande du film avec des acteurs du cru. Heureusement, Garbo parle allemand.

STILL FROM 'ANNA CHRISTIE' (GERMAN VERSION, 1930)
The costuming made it evident that Garbo played a prostitute, making her transformation more emphatic. / Garbos Kleidung zu Anfang unterstreicht, dass sie eine Prostituierte spielt, und so ist ihre Läuterung umso offensichtlicher. / Sa métamorphose est d'autant plus visible que les costumes rendent plus évident le fait qu'elle incarne une prostituée.

PAGES 104/105
ON THE SET OF 'ANNA CHRISTIE' (GERMAN VERSION, 1930)
Jacques Feyder directs with the ever-present William Daniels behind the camera. / Jacques Feyder führt Regie, während der allgegenwärtige William Daniels hinter der Kamera steht. / Sous la direction de Jacques Feyder, avec William Daniels derrière la caméra.

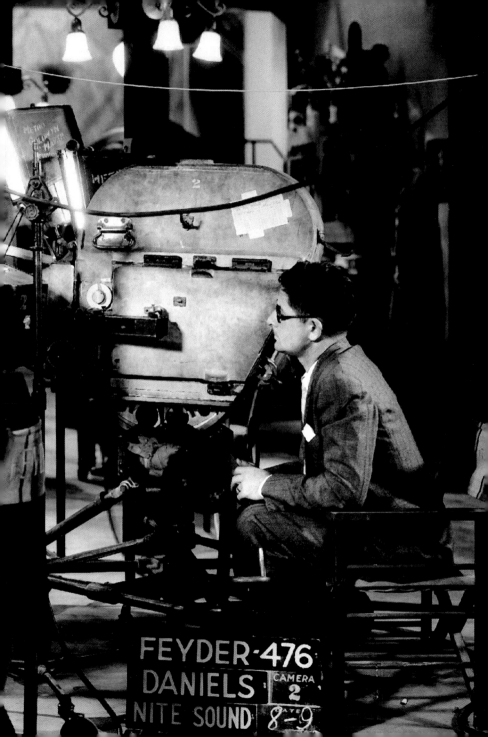

STILL FROM 'ROMANCE' (1930)
Gavin Gordon had a car accident on the way to the
studio on the first day of filming, then fainted when he
arrived – he had broken his shoulder. Eager to start
filming without delay, he left the hospital too early and
broke his shoulder again. / Auf dem Weg ins Studio
hatte Gavin Gordon am ersten Drehtag einen
Autounfall und fiel gleich bei seiner Ankunft in
Ohnmacht: Er hatte sich die Schulter gebrochen. Weil
er aber unbedingt mit den Dreharbeiten beginnen
wollte, verließ er das Krankenhaus zu früh und brach
sich die Schulter erneut. / Victime d'un accident de
voiture le premier jour du tournage, Gavin Gordon
s'évanouit en arrivant au studio, l'épaule fracturée.
Soucieux de ne pas retarder le film, il quitte trop tôt
l'hôpital et se fracture à nouveau l'épaule.

PORTRAIT FOR 'ROMANCE' (1930)
For each film the studio usually arranged for a top
photographer to take portraits of the stars. After this
session with George Hurrell, which she considered a
disaster, she only worked with Clarence Sinclair Bull. /
Das Studio engagierte üblicherweise für jeden Film
einen Spitzenfotografen, um die Stars zu porträtieren.
Nach dieser Sitzung mit George Hurrell, die ihrer
Ansicht nach katastrophal verlief, arbeitete Garbo nur
noch mit Clarence Sinclair Bull. / Pour chaque film, le
studio demande à un grand photographe de tirer le
portrait des vedettes. Après cette séance avec George
Hurrell, qu'elle considère comme un désastre, Garbo ne
travaillera plus qu'avec Clarence Sinclair Bull.

STILL FROM 'ROMANCE' (1930)
Garbo played an Italian soprano who spoke fractured
English. She lip-synched the two arias but spoke her
own dialogue. / Garbo spielt eine italienische
Sopranistin, die gebrochen Englisch spricht. Ihre beiden
Arien mimte sie zum Playback, aber ihren Text sprach
sie selbst. / Garbo incarne une soprano italienne
maîtrisant mal l'anglais. Elle chante les deux airs en playback mais enregistre elle-même les dialogues.

PORTRAIT FOR 'ROMANCE' (1930)
Garbo's 'look' was influential throughout America.
Department stores reported increased sales of false
eyelashes to replicate her long lashes, as well as the
clothes she wore, especially berets and cloche hats. /
Garbos „Look" beeinflusste ganz Amerika. In den
Warenhäusern boomte der Absatz von falschen
Augenlidern (mit denen man ihre echten nachahmen
konnte) und Garbo-Outfits, insbesondere von
Baskenmützen und Glockenhüten. / Le look de Garbo
déteint sur l'Amérique. Les grands magasins voient
s'envoler les ventes de faux cils et de vêtements
affectionnés par la star, en particulier les bérets et les
chapeaux cloches.

STILL FROM 'INSPIRATION' (1931)
As with 'Romance,' Garbo had been reluctant to make the film but was talked into it. / Wie schon im Falle von *Romanze* zögerte Garbo anfänglich, ließ sich dann aber zu diesem Film überreden. / Comme pour *Romance*, Garbo s'est fait prier avant d'accepter le rôle.

ON THE SET OF 'INSPIRATION' (1931)
There was silent conflict between director Clarence Brown (in front of camera) and Garbo because he wanted rehearsals for the actors while she wanted to complete the scene on the first take, without on-set rehearsal. / Im Stillen brodelte es zwischen Regisseur Clarence Brown (vor der Kamera) und Garbo, weil er wollte, dass die Schauspieler proben, sie hingegen wollte die Szene gleich beim ersten Durchlauf „im Kasten" haben. / Un sourd antagonisme oppose Garbo au réalisateur Clarence Brown (devant la caméra): alors qu'il tient à faire répéter les acteurs, elle aime boucler la scène dès la première prise.

PAGES 112/113
STILL FROM 'INSPIRATION' (1931)
Garbo played a Parisian prostitute who is the inspiration for poets, artists, sculptors and writers. / Garbo spielt eine Pariser Prostituierte, die Dichter, Künstler, Bildhauer und Schriftsteller inspiriert. / Garbo incarne une prostituée parisienne qui sert de muse aux poètes, aux peintres, aux sculpteurs et aux écrivains.

STILL FROM 'INSPIRATION' (1931)
Robert Montgomery revealed that working with Garbo did not necessarily constitute an introduction to her – she did not talk to him off the set. / Robert Montgomery wies darauf hin, dass die Zusammenarbeit mit Garbo nicht notwendigerweise bedeutete, dass man wusste, wer sie war – außerhalb der Kulissen wechselte sie mit ihm kein Wort. / Comme le souligne Robert Montgomery, travailler avec Garbo ne permet pas forcément de la connaître, car elle ne lui adresse pas la parole hors du plateau.

PORTRAIT FOR 'INSPIRATION' (1931)
As with several of her weaker films, the critics pointed out the faults of the director and writer, but had nothing but praise for Garbo's performance. / Wie auch bei einigen anderen ihrer schwächeren Filme, wiesen die Kritiker auf Fehler bei Drehbuch und Regie hin, waren aber voll des Lobes für Garbos schauspielerische Leistung. / Comme pour plusieurs de ses films mineurs, la critique relève les défauts de la réalisation et du scénario, mais ne trouve rien à redire au jeu de l'actrice.

STILL FROM 'SUSAN LENOX (HER FALL AND RISE)' (1931)
Garbo plays a girl who flees when she is menaced by Jeb (Alan Hale). / Garbo spielt ein Mädchen, das von Jeb (Alan Hale) bedroht wird, und deshalb fortläuft. / Menacée par Alan Hale, la jeune héroïne s'enfuit.

"There is no one who would have me ...
I can't cook."
Greta Garbo

„Mich würde keiner haben wollen ... Ich kann nicht kochen."
Greta Garbo

« Personne ne voudrait de moi ... Je ne sais pas cuisiner. »
Greta Garbo

STILL FROM 'SUSAN LENOX (HER FALL AND RISE)' (1931)
The runaway finds security with Rodney (Clark Gable). The film follows Garbo as she makes money from men but falls morally. / Die Ausreißerin flüchtet sich in die Arme von Rodney Spencer (Clark Gable). Der Film folgt Susan, die durch Männer zu Geld kommt, aber moralisch verkommt. / La fugitive trouve refuge auprès de Clark Gable. Si les hommes font sa fortune, ils l'entraîneront également à sa perte.

PAGES 118/119
ON THE SET OF 'SUSAN LENOX (HER FALL AND RISE)' (1931)
MGM protected their stars. 22 writers worked on this film, Garbo walked out six times until the script was fixed, and Robert Z. Leonard (center) directed retakes. It went on to be a hit worldwide. / MGM stellte sich hinter seine Stars. Obwohl 22 Autoren an dem Drehbuch feilten, verließ Garbo sechsmal das Set, bis alles stimmte. Robert Z. Leonard (Mitte) führte bei den Nachdrehs Regie. Am Ende wurde der Film zu einem Welterfolg. / La MGM soigne ses stars. Bien que 22 scénaristes soient sur le pont, Garbo claquera six fois la porte avant d'accepter le script. La seconde version sera la bonne et le film fera un tabac.

STILL FROM 'SUSAN LENOX (HER FALL AND RISE)' (1931)
Garbo's redemption in the film comes when she sacrifices herself for Gable. / Susan (Garbo) findet ihre Erlösung, als sie sich für Rodney (Gable) opfert. / Dans ce film, Garbo trouve la rédemption en se sacrifiant pour Gable.

PAGE 122
PORTRAIT FOR 'MATA HARI' (1931)
A stunning and improbable dress for spy Mata Hari, designed by Adrian. / Ein ebenso gewagtes wie unmögliches Kleid für die Spionin Mata Hari, entworfen von Adrian. / Dans le costume ahurissant dessiné par Adrian pour l'espionne Mata Hari.

STILL FROM 'SUSAN LENOX (HER FALL AND RISE)' (1931)
Garbo always sold better abroad than in America. / Garbo verkaufte sich in Übersee stets besser als in Amerika. / Garbo se vendra toujours mieux à l'étranger qu'en Amérique.

PAGE 123
STILL FROM 'MATA HARI' (1931)
Garbo seduces Roman Navarro so that she can steal war secrets – the sex scenes had to be censored. / Garbo verführt den Leutnant (Ramón Novarro), um in den Besitz von Kriegsgeheimnissen zu gelangen. Die Sexszenen fielen der Zensur zum Opfer. / Garbo séduit Ramón Novarro pour lui dérober des secrets de guerre, mais les scènes érotiques sont censurées.

"Her emotional intensity is genuine. The instant she
begins a scene, her whole being seems to change.
Her role acts as a complete metamorphosis.
At once she is Mata Hari and not Greta Garbo.
It is an inspiration to work with her. You find
yourself living the role, not merely acting it."

Ramón Novarro

„Ihre emotionale Intensität ist echt. In dem
Augenblick, in dem sie eine Szene beginnt,
scheint sich ihr gesamtes Wesen zu verändern.
Ihre Rolle bewirkt eine vollkommene Verwandlung –
augenblicklich ist sie Mata Hari und nicht mehr
Greta Garbo. Mit ihr zu arbeiten, ist eine
Inspiration. Plötzlich lebt man die Rolle,
man spielt sie nicht mehr nur."

Ramón Novarro

« Son intensité émotionnelle est authentique.
Dès qu'une scène commence, elle se transforme
entièrement. Son rôle opère une complète
métamorphose. Elle devient soudain Mata Hari
et non plus Greta Garbo. C'est une source
d'inspiration de travailler avec elle. On se met à
vivre le rôle, et non plus seulement à le jouer. »

Ramón Novarro

STILL FROM 'MATA HARI' (1931)
In the most controversial scene, Garbo asks Novarro
to extinguish a votive candle for his mother before they
make love. In some cinemas, the candle was replaced
with a picture of his mother. / In der umstrittensten
Szene bittet Mata Hari (Garbo) den Leutnant (Novarro)
vor dem Liebesakt, eine Votivkerze für seine Mutter zu
löschen. In einigen Kinos lief eine Fassung, in der die
Kerze durch ein Bild der Mutter ersetzt worden war. /
Dans la scène la plus controversée, Garbo demande à
Novarro d'éteindre la bougie allumée à la mémoire de sa
mère avant de faire l'amour. Dans certains cinémas,
la bougie est remplacée par une photo de sa mère.

STILL FROM 'GRAND HOTEL' (1932)
Garbo plays a Russian ballerina who has lost her desire
to perform. She is a guest in the Grand Hotel, and her
story is just one of many told in this portmanteau film
full of stars. / Garbo spielt eine russische Ballerina, die
ihre Lust am Tanzen verloren hat. Sie wohnt im Grand
Hotel, und ihre Geschichte ist eine von vielen, die in
diesem, mit zahlreichen großen Stars besetzten Film
erzählt wird. / Garbo, qui incarne une ballerine russe
ayant perdu la vocation, séjourne au Grand Hôtel au
milieu d'une kyrielle de stars dont chacune a son
histoire.

PAGES 128/129
STILL FROM 'GRAND HOTEL' (1932)
Garbo worked from 9am to 5pm, and Joan Crawford
worked from 5pm to 2am. The production was all held
together by director Edmund Goulding, who brought
out the feminine characteristics of his stars. / Garbo
arbeitete von 9 bis 17 Uhr und Joan Crawford von 17 bis
2 Uhr. Zusammengehalten wurde das Ganze von
Regisseur Edmund Goulding, der die feminine
Ausstrahlung seiner Stars hervorhob. / Garbo travaille
de 9 h à 17 h et Joan Crawford de 17 h à 2 h du matin. La
cohésion est assurée par le réalisateur, Edmund
Goulding, qui fait ressortir la féminité des actrices.

PAGE 130
STILL FROM 'GRAND HOTEL' (1932)
Garbo helped rearrange the set furniture so that costar
John Barrymore could have his favoured left profile. /
Garbo half, die Möbel am Set so zu arrangieren, dass ihr
Filmpartner John Barrymore vorteilhaft von links zu
sehen war. / Garbo aide à réaménager le plateau de
manière à ce que son partenaire, John Barrymore,
puisse présenter son meilleur profil.

PAGE 131
**ARTICLE IN 'THE NEW MOVIE MAGAZINE'
(AUGUST 1933)**
The fan magazines delighted in finding new ways to
feature the stars. / Die Fanzeitschriften hatten Spaß
daran, die Stars immer wieder von einer anderen Seite
zu zeigen. / Les magazines rivalisent d'inventivité pour
évoquer les stars.

Picking the Winners
in the Type-sketch Game

*Portraits of Greta Garbo, made on
the typewriter, selected as the best*

Above: The photograph of Greta Garbo
that appeared in the May issue of The
New Movie Magazine, from which many
readers made strikingly good likenesses
on their typewriters.

★

At right: The type-sketch made by Harry
D. Reese, 5514 West Washington Boule-
vard, Chicago, Ill., selected as the best
of all submitted.

★

**For full details of the
Type-sketch awards
please turn to page 80**

At left: The type-sketch
made by Ray Erlen-
born, picked as the
second best, and (at
right) the type-sketch
made by Alicia J.
Spaulding, 632 Norfolk
Avenue, Buffalo, N. Y.,
named as one of the
ten next best.

42

The New Movie Magazine, August, 1933

"During these scenes I allow only the cameraman and lighting man on the set. The director goes out for a coffee or a milkshake. When people are watching, I'm just a woman making faces for the camera. It destroys the illusion. If I am by myself, my face will do things I cannot do with it otherwise."
Greta Garbo

„Während dieser Szenen erlaube ich nur dem Kameramann und den Beleuchtern, sich am Set aufzuhalten. Der Regisseur geht raus und trinkt einen Kaffee oder einen Milchshake. Wenn mir Leute zusehen, bin ich nur eine Frau, die für die Kamera Grimassen schneidet. Das zerstört die Illusion. Nur wenn ich allein bin, tut mein Gesicht die Dinge, die ich sonst nicht machen kann."
Greta Garbo

« Pendant ces scènes, je n'autorise que le chef opérateur et l'éclairagiste à rester sur le plateau. Le réalisateur va boire un café ou un milk-shake. S'il y a des gens qui me regardent, je ne suis qu'une femme en train de faire des grimaces devant la caméra. Cela détruit l'illusion. Si je suis seule, mon visage fait des choses que je ne sais pas faire autrement. »
Greta Garbo

STILL FROM 'AS YOU DESIRE ME' (1932)
Garbo plays a woman without a past. / Garbo spielt eine Frau ohne Vergangenheit. / Garbo incarne une femme sans passé.

STILL FROM 'AS YOU DESIRE ME' (1932)
Garbo insisted that Erich von Stroheim play the master
manipulator who turns her into the cabaret star Zara.
Stroheim was recovering from surgery and required
many takes, so Garbo took the blame to protect him. /
Garbo bestand darauf, dass Erich von Stroheim den
großen Manipulator spielte, der sie in den Kabarettstar
Zara verwandelt. Stroheim erholte sich gerade von
einem chirurgischen Eingriff und musste seine Szenen
oft wiederholen, doch Garbo nahm die Schuld dafür auf
sich, um ihn zu schützen. / Garbo insiste pour que le
rôle du manipulateur qui la transforme en vedette de
cabaret soit confié à Erich von Stroheim. Lorsque
l'acteur, convalescent, est contraint de multiplier les
prises, elle prend la responsabilité sur elle pour le
couvrir.

ON THE SET OF 'AS YOU DESIRE ME' (1932)
This set photo shows how back projection gives the
impression of being on location without leaving the
studio. / Dieses Foto zeigt, wie man durch eine
Rückprojektion eine Außenaufnahme vortäuscht, ohne
das Studio verlassen zu müssen. / Cette photo montre
comment les rétroprojections donnent l'illusion d'être
en extérieur sans quitter le studio.

PAGES 136/137
**ARTICLE IN 'HOLLYWOOD MAGAZINE'
(DECEMBER 1933)**
Interviews with Garbo were rare, and they became
much more so when she visited Sweden for nine
months. / Interviews mit Garbo waren ohnehin eine
Rarität, zumal während ihrer neunmonatigen Schweden-
reise. / Les interviews de Garbo sont une denrée rare,
surtout lorsqu'elle retourne passer neuf mois en Suède.

GARBO'S

Greta Garbo's sphinx-like silence is lifted as, for the first time, she discusses herself and her admirers and forcefully reveals the reasons for her trip to Sweden!

"I WANT TO REST," said Greta Garbo in a low voice. And then, after a dramatic pause, she added, "if there is any rest for a restless soul."

She stared, almost defiantly, at the circle of Swedish and English newspapermen gathered around her. Prompted by her attitude, by the timidity with which she had approached the waiting interviewers, one of them asked:

"Do you think the press is dangerous?"

Garbo shook her head negatively.

"I don't know that I have anything against the press," she replied. "But I do think that much of what is written is unnecessary. What does it profit all the magazines and newspapers that they describe how I eat and drink and when I go to bed? Whether I sew and—oh, I don't know—"

She spread her hands expressively.

"My work is inside the studio. Why the public should be interested in my private life I can't understand. And I don't think that contact between the public and the film player does any good. It distracts her from her work. Therefore, I eliminate the public. But that doesn't mean that I am not thankful for the interest the public has in me. I am not ungrateful. I would like to thank everyone personally but if I were to do that, my next film probably would be bad—and that I will not have. But there is one interest in me that I am not thankful for—"

"And that is?"

"All this interest devoted to me by men and woman who write about me in their magazines. I'll tell you how it works out. I have never written any articles for a magazine. I have yet to sit down and relate my life's history to a newspaperman. And yet I read words that supposedly came from own mouth, concerning Goethe and Wagner and love and Gandhi."

She smiled, a bit appealingly, her eyes wide.

"You understand if I am a little aggravated by journalists. But of course I can't be categorical. That would be the same as to judge a nation because a few representatives of that nation haven't acted fairly."

She again gave a negative shake of her head when asked if she intended to make pictures in Sweden and if she would purchase Ivar Kreuger's summer home. Since then it has been reported that she did buy the match king's $150,000 home, paying only $10,000 for the estate.

"I don't know," she replied to the questions. "I haven't any plans. No, I do know one thing. I am not going to buy Kreuger's villa."

A few more idle questions, a growing impatience on the part of Garbo and the interview was over. She arose, flashed a warm, schoolgirl smile, a purely natural little gesture, and departed in the company of her brother, Sven Gustafsson.

DURING THE INTERVIEW the writer studied her, comparing her with the Garbo he had seen when last she came home. Wearing a yellow golf jumper, gray skirt, gray, low-heeled shoes, gray béret set jauntily on her head, and a gray cape, she was a bit pale and looked tired under the eyes as she arrived for the interview.

The sober, weary Garbo now seeking solitude and rest in her beloved Sweden is in striking contrast to the happy girl who visited her home in 1929

HOLLYWOOD

First Interview!

by PETER JOEL
Well-known Swedish writer

"I want to rest," said Garbo in a low voice, adding dramatically, "if there is any rest for a restless soul." This unusual picture was made during her recent interview

Garbo curtly said "No!" and slammed the door when a New York reporter asked for an interview aboard the boat. Later the interviewer learned she had awakened Garbo from a much needed sleep for which powders had been taken

She spoke with a weariness that gave force to her statement that all she wanted was to rest. That some of the men wondered if she were acting or really meant what she said is not strange for there was a marked difference in this interview as compared with the one granted in 1929 when she arrived in Sweden for a visit.

In 1929 she was happy, almost gay, when Swedish reporters boarded the ship to talk with her. She laughed and chatted merrily. It was apparent, then, that she found enjoyment in being bombarded with questions. It was fun to get home; to find her mother and brother waiting for her.

During the ocean voyage on that trip home she had taken part in the social life of the ship. She went to the bar for a cocktail before dinner and talked pleasantly with the bartender. Life was interesting and Garbo was natural. On this last voyage, however, she spent most of her

time in her stateroom. The majority of her meals were served to her in private and she permitted the other passengers to catch only a glimpse of her. She endured, rather than enjoyed, the voyage.

There was a marked contrast in her meeting with reporters, too. This time the newspapermen were not at all sure they would get an interview. There had been many stories about the manner in which she was to escape meeting the public. But the interview was granted and the newspapermen, watching for changes that had been wrought in her, looked at her sharply when she appeared. If Garbo seemed to draw back a little it may have been because she realized they were judging her. Judging her in the rôle of Swede as well as newspapermen; judging with a knowledge of Sweden and Swedes.

She appeared "a shrinking little creature with something of the air of a martyr about to be cast to the lions," as one of the men later said.

After the interview was concluded a little incident

Please turn to page fifty

STILL FROM 'QUEEN CHRISTINA' (1933)
Garbo researched, accessed secret files, and made
sketches of costumes, furniture and architecture to do
justice to her Swedish queen. / Um der Rolle der
schwedischen Königin gerecht zu werden, recherchierte
Greta Garbo, verschaffte sich Zugang zu geheimen
Dokumenten und fertigte Skizzen von Kostümen,
Mobiliar und Gebäuden. / Garbo entreprend des
recherches, accède à des dossiers secrets et trace des
croquis des costumes, des meubles et de l'architecture
pour rendre honneur à la reine de Suède.

PAGES 140/141
STILL FROM 'QUEEN CHRISTINA' (1933)
After Garbo and Gilbert make love, she wanders the
room to memorise it forever. This sequence gave
anxiety to the censors, but the film was released intact
and made $2.5 million worldwide. / Nachdem Kristina
(Garbo) und Antonio (John Gilbert) den Liebesakt
vollzogen haben, prägt sie sich jede Einzelheit des
Zimmers ein. Der Zensur war diese Szene zu erotisch,
doch sie wurde nicht geschnitten, und der Film spielte
weltweit 2,5 Millionen US-Dollar ein. / Après avoir fait
l'amour avec Gilbert, Garbo parcourt la pièce pour la
mémoriser à jamais. Malgré la désapprobation de la
censure, le film est laissé intact et rapporte 2,5 millions
de dollars dans le monde.

STILL FROM 'QUEEN CHRISTINA' (1933)
She also enjoyed dressing as a man, giving a sexual
ambiguity to the film. / Es machte ihr Spaß, sich als
Mann zu verkleiden, wodurch der Film eine sexuelle
Doppeldeutigkeit bekam. / Elle se plaît à s'habiller en
homme, conférant ainsi une ambiguïté sexuelle au film.

*"Her independence of either sex is responsible for
the cryptic amorality of her performances."*
Kenneth Tynan

*„Ihre Unabhängigkeit von beiden Geschlechtern ist
verantwortlich für die rätselhafte Amoralität ihres
Spiels."*
Kenneth Tynan

*« Son indépendance vis-à-vis des deux sexes
explique l'étrange amoralité de son jeu. »*
Kenneth Tynan

PAGES 142/143
ON THE SET OF 'QUEEN CHRISTINA' (1933)
When her lover (John Gilbert) dies the film ends with
a long close-up of Garbo's face – one of the great
moments of her career – here captured by William
Daniels and director Rouben Mamoulian. / Nach
Antonios Tod endet der Film mit einer langen
Nahaufnahme von Garbos Gesicht – einer der großen
Augenblicke ihrer Karriere, festgehalten von William
Daniels und Regisseur Rouben Mamoulian. / À la mort
de John Gilbert, le film s'achève sur un gros plan du
visage de Garbo – l'un des grands moments de sa
carrière, immortalisé par William Daniels et le
réalisateur Rouben Mamoulian.

STILL FROM 'THE PAINTED VEIL' (1934)
Head electrician Floyd Porter followed Garbo around
the set with a key light aimed at her eyes, to give them a
sparkle. It was her custom to tap Floyd on the shoulder
every time she left the set. / Oberbeleuchter Floyd
Porter folgte Garbo auf Schritt und Tritt mit einer
Lampe, die auf ihre Augen gerichtet war, um sie zum
Glänzen zu bringen. Garbo hatte die Angewohnheit,
Floyd jedes Mal auf die Schulter zu klopfen, wenn sie
das Set verließ. / Le chef électricien Floyd Porter suit
Garbo en braquant une lumière sur ses yeux pour les
faire briller. En quittant le plateau, elle a pour coutume
de lui taper sur l'épaule.

PAGES 146/147
ARTICLE IN 'PHOTOPLAY' (OCTOBER 1934)

PORTRAIT FOR 'THE PAINTED VEIL' (1934)
During the preview audiences laughed at Garbo's
otherworldly costumes. / Während der
Testvorführungen lachte das Publikum über Garbos
weltfremde Kostüme. / Lors des avant-premières,
le public rit de ses costumes étranges.

GARBO
Starts
Her New
Picture

"TAKE 1"—which means the first scene in Greta's new Metro-Goldwyn-Mayer film, "The Painted Veil." The first call of "Camera!" for a Garbo picture is always a thrilling second. This time it stirred more excitement, more speculation than ever before. The great Swedish star's M-G-M contract ends with this production. What will she do? What will M-G-M do? Well, perhaps much depends on the public's verdict. Is Garbo still the queen? Will the public like the adaptation of this Somerset Maugham novel, about man's battle against cholera in the Chinese interior, and a woman starved for love through her doctor-husband's zeal for his work? It should, for Garbo never fails. The great one, as *Katherine Koeber*, is displaying some silk stockings to her sister, *Olga*, who is preparing for her honeymoon. The sister rôle, second most important in the picture, was coveted by many of Hollywood's younger actresses, but finally entrusted to Cecilia Parker, just graduating from Westerns and serials. Richard Boleslavsky, directing Garbo for the first time, reclines on the floor in his worn leather jacket, with his inevitable pipe. William Daniels, head cameraman for the celebrated Scandinavian in all her American pictures, sits pensively on the stepladder, left foreground. His assistant, Al Lane, is at the camera controls. (The electrician, standing in the background, also has worked on all of Garbo's productions.) All of the sets for "The Painted Veil" were constructed on stilts, as this photograph reveals. The set has a ceiling, which is unusual from a scenic angle.—*Photo by Milton Brown*

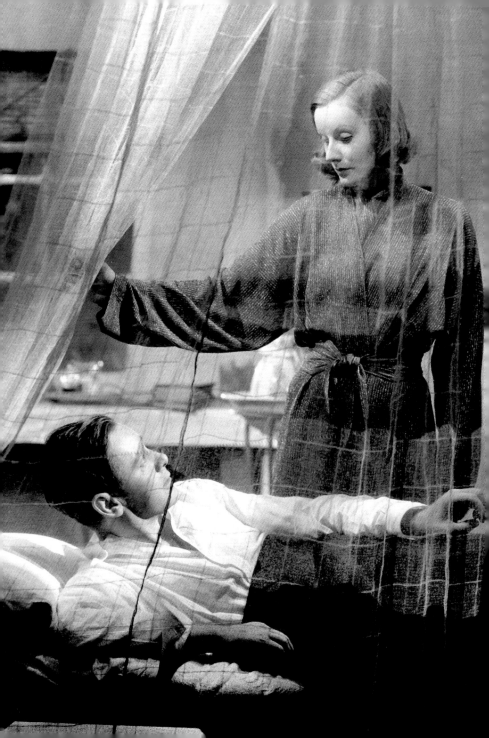

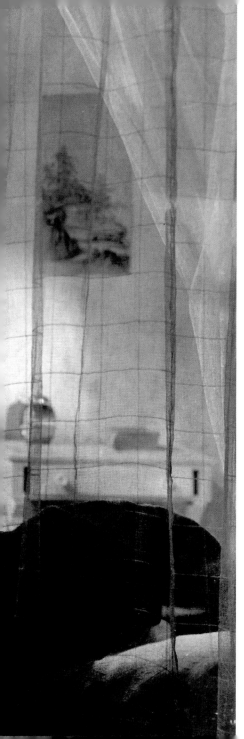

STILL FROM 'THE PAINTED VEIL' (1934)
Garbo marries bacteriologist Herbert Marshall (in bed)
and has an affair with George Brent, but only grows to
love her husband when he is wounded. / Katrin Koerber
(Garbo) heiratet den Bakteriologen Dr. Fane (Herbert
Marshall, im Bett) und hat eine Liebesaffäre mit Jack
Townsend (George Brent). Erst, als ihr Ehemann
verletzt wird, lernt sie ihn lieben. / Après avoir épousé
le bactériologiste Herbert Marshall (allongé), Garbo le
trompe avec George Brent et ne s'éprend de lui
qu'après maintes mésaventures.

PAGES 150/151
**ARTICLE IN 'THE NEW MOVIE MAGAZINE'
(APRIL 1935)**
With Garbo rarely giving interviews, it was common for
the fan magazines to feature interviews with people
who had met her, however briefly. / Da Garbo selbst
selten Interviews gab, druckten die Fanzeitschriften
häufig Interviews mit Personen, die sie irgendwann
einmal kennen gelernt hatten – und sei es auch noch so
flüchtig. / Faute de pouvoir interviewer la star, les
magazines s'évertuent à publier des entretiens avec des
personnes qui l'ont rencontrée, ne serait-ce que
brièvement.

PAGES 152/153
STILL FROM 'ANNA KARENINA' (1935)
Anna (Garbo) first meets Vronsky (Fredric March) at a
railway station, where a worker is accidentally crushed
by a train. It is an omen for their future together. / Anna
(Garbo) trifft Wronskij (Fredric March) zum ersten Mal
auf einem Bahnhof, als ein Arbeiter unter einen Zug
gerät: Der Unfall ist ein unheilvolles Omen für ihre
gemeinsame Zukunft. / Anna (Garbo) rencontre
Vronsky (Fredric March) dans une gare où un ouvrier
est accidentellement écrasé par un train, signe de
mauvais augure pour leur avenir commun.

James
Montgome
Flagg

CRETA CARBO

JAMES MONTGOMERY FLAGG

With   CONRAD   NAGEL . . . ROBERT   MONTGOMERY . . . CLARK   GABLE . . . CHARLES   BICKFORD . . . LEW   AYRE

James Montgomery Flagg Reveals
The GARBO YOU NEVER KNEW

**Continuing our series, of favorite stars of famous people, James Montgomery Flagg, famous illustrator, says,
"Garbo's face has as much character as Abraham Lincoln's has for a man. Fortitude! She's magnificent!"**

By DOUGLAS GILBERT

IT is the opinion of James Montgomery Flagg that Greta Garbo is the greatest of the film stars. The silent Swede, says the renowned artist, has everything. He places no crown on her golden head—but a halo. According to Mr. Flagg, Greta is greater than art.

It sounds like a Hollywood rave. Moreover, to your correspondent who laid siege to Mr. Flagg in his New York studio for his selection, it was at first—a nuisance choice. I had never before contributed so much as a gram to the tons of tripe that weigh down the fabulous Garbo. And I hesitated, in the early stages of our interview, crestfallen at thus being forced to commit a violating act.

But, so help me, the Flagg Garbo is no one you have ever met before. She emerged through his summation, not the pseudo-sphinx shunning the quoted world, but a melancholy Swede, a mystery woman whose screwy reactions, indeed, rudeness, are born of sorrow. And I don't mean a yearning for the dead Stiller. It seems Mr. Flagg knows Garbo. Let us get to his characterization at once.

"She vibrates, does things to you. She has a terrific lot of dignity. She carries around with her a Swedish phonograph record of laughs; no words recorded, no music, just laughs—belly-laughs, hysterical chortles, loud guffaws, laughs that are insane, satiric, happy, derisive, sardonic—every degree of emotional response in laughter. Then she'll play it on her host's or hostess's phonograph and watch the reaction. I don't know what it means. . . ."

Perhaps I should explain that Mr. Flagg is picturing Miss Garbo after an all-afternoon social contact with her at a party given by a director some years ago when he was in Hollywood. She was Garbo in person. She was apparently at ease in his company and spoke, on the word of Mr. Flagg, with earnest freedom.

"We sat together on a sofa. I didn't find her aloof, reticent, or rude, as others are said to have found her. True, she wasn't voluble at the start. But something clicked in me when we met, and I have often wondered if she realized it too. Realized what it was. She certainly gave me the key at the start with an astonishing revelation. She confessed to me that she suffered from melancholia.

"Well, years ago as a youth, studying in England. I had been a victim of melancholia, and I was sympathetically bonded to her at once. This might well be a spiritual affinity. Moreover, she told me that she had experienced melancholy in her youth, so I discounted the stories I had heard of her sorrow for the dead Mauritz Stiller, her first director in Stockholm, and the man she is said to have loved—he who was responsible for her success.

"Success? I wondered just how much it meant to her. I recall how she characterized herself to me during her conversation; it was 'Svenska flicke,' which means, I believe, 'just a little Swedish girl.' While we were talking I asked her if she'd pose that I might sketch her. She agreed, graciously and with charming politeness, and I began to wonder again at the tales I had heard of her rudeness.

"She tilted back her head, revealing her lean neck, which is one of the most remarkable characteristics of her features, and I began. I was interested, tremendously interested, and took some pains to make a finished drawing, not just a hasty sketch. I said, 'you are tired?' And she said, 'no, I am not tired. You are the first real artist I have met in America.' It shut me up, for a moment. But she never betrayed the slightest sign of kidding me. She really sounded very sincere. I finished the sketch and gave it to John Gilbert.

"Then I did something unpardonable, and to this day I can't tell you why. I reached down, picked up her tea-cup, and drank from it. She looked at me for a moment, steadily, with just a trace of disdain. She said, 'Are those American manners?' I would have given an arm not to have had it happen. Yet it was worth seeing her coldness, an indescribable frozen contempt.

"Millions admire her I know. I'm not traveling with the herd; I just think they have good taste. And another thing, she hasn't got big feet, it's all damn nonsense. She's tall, about five feet six inches; if her feet were smaller they'd be disproportionate. And her face to me has as much character as Abraham Lincoln's has for a man. My feeling for her art is best summed up in her final scene in 'Queen Christina.' I shall

never forget her bravery as she goes forth, standing there at the prow of her ship—such fortitude, such utter renunciation. She is magnificent."

Says Mr. Flagg. Now let's take a breather and get down to case histories. Frankly, I am at a loss to understand Mr. Flagg's rave. So far as I know he has never committed himself to superlatives with such abandon before. Indeed, as a forthright artist in New York for some forty years, he has always insisted upon calling a spade a spade and not a "garden implement." Now he goes haywire over Garbo.

I suspect that his affection for her artistry is more than "a melancholy affinity." They have more in common than that. Like Garbo, Flagg shuns the multitude. Both run on independent tickets. Both are courageous, Garbo shrewdly silent in her fortitude, Flagg with outspokenness. He once characterized the nation, indignantly commenting upon some mass response, as "the United Sheep of America."

He is really one of the remarkable characters of commercial art, so prolific he was once accused of being a syndicate. His was no beginner's career. He was in the money almost from the start, earning when sixteen, a stipend for his drawings for *Life*, *St. Nicholas* and other magazines that would be a fairish figure today.

A native of New York born of New England stock, he studied in art schools for six years; all wasted time, he says, "unless I had gone to college in which case the time wasted would have been appalling." There is less nonsense about Flagg than almost any other commercial artist. Is the illustrator's field art or business? Flagg will tell you —business. Says it has to be so in an industrial nation where a man is appraised by what he earns or what he earns.

He has no highfalutin' views about art for art's sake. A publisher of educational (*Please turn to page 63*)

The list of Greta's leading-men is staggering. See the photographs below.

With JOHN GILBERT . . . HERBERT MARSHALL . . . RAMON NOVARRO . . . JOHN BARRYMORE . . . and GEORGE

STILL FROM 'ANNA KARENINA' (1935)
Anna is married but openly flirts with Vronsky at a
garden party in front of their friends. / Anna ist zwar
verheiratet, flirtet aber bei einem Gartenfest vor ihren
Freunden ganz offen mit Wronskij. / Bien que mariée,
Anna flirte ouvertement avec Vronsky sous les yeux de
leurs amis lors d'une garden-party.

PORTRAIT FOR 'ANNA KARENINA' (1935)
Garbo reputedly ate garlic to dissuade March's
advances during their love scenes. However, she was
probably following a new diet. She was always changing
her dietary habits. / Garbo soll angeblich Knoblauch
gegessen haben, um March während der Liebesszenen
auf Abstand zu halten. Vielleicht war sie aber auch
gerade auf einer neuen Diät, denn sie änderte ständig
ihre Essgewohnheiten. / La légende veut que Garbo
mange de l'ail pour repousser les avances de March
durant les scènes d'amour. En réalité, il s'agit sans doute
d'un de ses nouveaux régimes dont elle change
constamment.

STILL FROM 'ANNA KARENINA' (1935)
Even though Basil Rathbone, who played her husband,
had met Garbo previously, she did not acknowledge
that they knew each other. / Obwohl Basil Rathbone,
der ihren Ehemann spielte, Garbo schon früher
getroffen hatte, gab sie nicht zu, dass sie sich kannten. /
Bien que Basil Rathbone, qui interprète son mari, ait
déjà rencontré Garbo, elle ne fait aucune allusion au fait
qu'ils se connaissent.

"Greta Garbo had something that nobody ever
had on the screen. [...] I would take a scene with
Garbo – pretty good. I would take it three or four
times. It was pretty good, but I was never quite
satisfied. When I saw that same scene on the
screen, however, it had something that it just didn't
have on the set. Garbo had something behind the
eyes that you couldn't see until you'd
photographed it in close-up. You could see
thought."
Clarence Brown, director

STILL FROM 'ANNA KARENINA' (1935)
Garbo tried hard to establish a rapport with Freddie
Bartholomew. / Garbo bemühte sich sehr um ein gutes
Verhältnis zu Freddie Bartholomew. / Garbo s'efforce
d'être en harmonie avec le jeune Freddie Bartholomew.

„Greta Garbo besaß etwas, das niemand auf der
Leinwand je hatte. [...] Ich drehte eine Szene mit
Garbo – ganz gut. Ich drehte drei oder vier Takes.
Es war recht gut, aber ich war nie ganz zufrieden.
Aber wenn ich die gleiche Szene auf der Leinwand
sah, dann hatte sie das, was am Set fehlte. Hinter
Garbos Augen verbarg sich etwas, das man nicht
sehen konnte, bis man es in Nahaufnahme filmte.
Dann sah man ihre Gedanken.“
Clarence Brown, Regisseur

« Greta Garbo possédait une qualité que personne
d'autre n'a jamais eue à l'écran. [...] Je tournais une
scène avec elle et ce n'était pas mal. Je refaisais
trois ou quatre prises. C'était bien, mais je n'étais
pas tout à fait satisfait. Cependant, quand je
revoyais la même scène à l'écran, il s'en dégageait
une impression qui n'était pas perceptible sur le
plateau. Garbo avait quelque chose dans le regard
qui n'apparaissait qu'une fois photographié en gros
plan. On pouvait lire dans ses pensées. »
Clarence Brown, réalisateur

STILL FROM 'ANNA KARENINA' (1935)
The train takes Anna to a predetermined destination, relentless and uncaring. / Der Zug bringt Anna zu einem vorbestimmten Ort – unweigerlich und erbarmungslos. / Le train emporte inexorablement Anna vers son destin.

PAGES 160/161
ON THE SET OF 'CAMILLE' (1936)
George Cukor (standing by camera) directs Garbo and Robert Taylor in this classic story of doomed love. / Garbo und Robert Taylor spielen unter der Regie von George Cukor (neben der Kamera stehend) in dieser klassischen Geschichte einer Liebe, die zum Scheitern verurteilt ist. / George Cukor (debout près de la caméra) dirige Garbo et Robert Taylor dans cette grande histoire d'amour vouée à l'échec.

PORTRAIT FOR 'ANNA KARENINA' (1935)
This portrait evokes Anna's solitary life. The bars are like a cage. / Dieses Porträt suggeriert Annas Einsamkeit. Die Stäbe wirken wie ein Käfig. / Ce portrait, dont les barreaux évoquent ceux d'une cage, traduit la solitude de l'héroïne.

STILL FROM 'CAMILLE' (1936)
Three versions of the death scene were filmed. Garbo: "If you're going to die on screen, you've got to be strong and in good health." / Der Tod wurde in drei verschiedenen Versionen gedreht. Garbo: „Wenn man im Film stirbt, muss man stark und bei guter Gesundheit sein." / Garbo, qui a tourné trois versions de la scène finale, déclare que «pour mourir à l'écran, il faut être fort et en bonne santé».

STILL FROM 'CAMILLE' (1936)
In the role of Camille, Garbo was cool on the surface but seething with reckless sexual energy underneath. She was nominated for an Oscar. / In der Rolle der Camille wirkte Garbo nach außen kühl, aber unter der Oberfläche brodelte eine unverhüllte sexuelle Kraft. Sie wurde für einen Oscar nominiert. / Sous son apparente froideur, Garbo (qui sera sélectionnée aux Oscars) déborde de sensualité torride.

PAGES 164/165
STILL FROM 'CONQUEST' (1937)
After the death of Irving Thalberg, MGM were inclined to spend money on sets and costumes rather than on scripts. / Nach Irving Thalbergs Tod gab MGM lieber Geld für Ausstattung und Kostüme als für Drehbücher aus. / Après la mort d'Irving Thalberg, la MGM décide d'investir dans les décors et les costumes plutôt que dans les scénarios.

STILL FROM 'CONQUEST' (1937)
Garbo plays an adulteress for the fourth time in
successive films. This time her lover was Napoléon,
played by Charles Boyer. / Garbo spielt zum vierten Mal
in Folge eine Ehebrecherin. Diesmal mimte Charles
Boyer ihren Liebhaber, Kaiser Napoléon. / Garbo, qui
incarne pour la quatrième fois de suite une femme
adultère, a cette fois pour amant Charles Boyer dans le
rôle de Napoléon.

ON THE SET OF 'CONQUEST' (1937)
Clarence Brown always whispered his directions to
Garbo. The film took 127 days to make and lost the
studio $1.4 million. / Clarence Brown flüsterte Greta
Garbo seine Regieanweisungen stets ins Ohr. Die
Dreharbeiten für diesen Film dauerten 127 Tage, und
das Studio machte einen Verlust von 1,4 Millionen
US-Dollar. / Clarence Brown chuchote toujours ses
instructions à l'oreille de Garbo. Ce film, dont le
tournage dure 127 jours, fera perdre 1,4 million de
dollars à la MGM.

STILL FROM 'NINOTCHKA' (1939)
Garbo is a straightlaced humourless Soviet Communist
who falls in love with an American (Melvyn Douglas). /
Garbo spielt eine zugeknöpfte und humorlose
sowjetische Kommunistin, die sich in den Amerikaner
Leon (Melvyn Douglas) verliebt. / Garbo incarne une
communiste austère et coincée qui tombe amoureuse
de l'Américain Melvyn Douglas.

"I have never played with a woman with such an
ability to arouse the erotic impulse. The fact that
an actress lets her partner take her in his arms or
presses her lips against his does not make a love
scene. You have also to see the emotion that drives
her, and it is this that Garbo conjures at the right
moment."
Melvyn Douglas

„Ich habe nie an der Seite einer Frau gespielt, die
eine solche Fähigkeit besaß, den erotischen Impuls
zu wecken. Nur, weil eine Schauspielerin ihrem
Filmpartner gestattet, sie in seine Arme zu nehmen
oder sie ihre Lippen auf die seinen drückt, wird
daraus noch keine Liebesszene. Man muss die
Gefühle sehen, die sie dazu treiben, und das ist es,
was Garbo im richtigen Moment herbeizaubert."
Melvyn Douglas

STILL FROM 'NINOTCHKA' (1939)
Garbo laughs! Director Ernst Lubitsch picked out a card
from the second preview: "Great picture. Funniest thing
I ever saw. I laughed so hard I peed in my girlfriend's
hand." / Die Garbo lacht! Regisseur Ernst Lubitsch las
auf einer Bewertungskarte der zweiten Testvorführung:
„Großartiger Film. Das Lustigste, was ich je gesehen
habe. Ich musste so sehr lachen, dass ich in die Hand
meiner Freundin gepinkelt habe." / Garbo rit! Lors de la
deuxième avant-première, le réalisateur Ernst Lubitsch
retient ce commentaire : « Jamais rien vu d'aussi drôle.
J'ai tellement ri que j'en ai mouillé mon pantalon et la
main de ma petite amie. »

« Je n'ai jamais joué avec une femme aussi douée
pour éveiller des pulsions érotiques. Le fait qu'une
actrice laisse son partenaire la prendre dans ses
bras ou pose ses lèvres sur les siennes ne suffit pas
à faire une scène d'amour. Il faut aussi percevoir
l'émotion qui la transporte, et c'est ce que Garbo
laisse filtrer au bon moment. »
Melvyn Douglas

STILL FROM 'NINOTCHKA' (1939)
Garbo had been labelled 'box office poison' in 1938,
and with World War Two all the profitable foreign
markets were closed to MGM. However, the film still
managed to make $2.2 million and earned Garbo an
Oscar nomination. / Garbo war 1938 als „Kassengift"
gebrandmarkt worden, und durch den Zweiten
Weltkrieg blieben die Auslandsmärkte für MGM
verschlossen. Dennoch spielte der Film 2,2 Millionen
US-Dollar ein und brachte Garbo erneut eine Oscar-
Nominierung. / Bien que Garbo ait été qualifiée en 1938
de «poison du box-office» et que la guerre ait fait
perdre à la MGM tous les marchés rentables à
l'étranger, ce film rapporte 2,2 millions de dollars
et lui vaut une sélection aux Oscars.

STILL FROM 'NINOTCHKA' (1939)
In 1948 the release of the film in Italy was credited with
defeating the Communists in the elections. / Angeblich
war es der Tatsache, dass der Film 1948 endlich auch in
die italienischen Kinos kam, zu verdanken, dass die
Kommunisten dort die Wahlen verloren. / En 1948, on
attribue à la sortie de ce film en Italie la défaite des
communistes aux élections.

STILL FROM 'TWO-FACED WOMAN' (1941)
Melvyn Douglas is the husband she wants back. /
Melvyn Douglas spielt den Mann, den sie zurückerobern
möchte. / Melvyn Douglas dans le rôle de l'époux
volage.

STILL FROM 'TWO-FACED WOMAN' (1941)
Garbo rhumbas! Garbo plays a highly principled woman
whose husband runs out on her. She pretends to be her
more easy-going twin to win him back. / Die Garbo tanzt
Rumba! Garbo spielt eine Frau mit hehren Grundsätzen,
die von ihrem Ehemann verlassen wird. Um ihn zurück
zu gewinnen, spielt sie ihre lebenslustige Zwillings-
schwester. / Garbo danse la rumba! Dans le rôle d'une
femme respectable abandonnée par son mari, elle se
fait passer pour sa jumelle délurée pour le reconquérir.

174

ON THE SET OF 'TWO-FACED WOMAN' (1941)
Garbo waits patiently as the distance is measured
between her and the camera so that she is in focus.
The film set out to make Garbo seem like an ordinary
woman. They were filming with an unfinished script, and
there were many retakes, but nothing could save the
film. / Garbo wartet geduldig, bis die Entfernung
zwischen ihr und der Kamera ausgemessen ist, um die
Bildschärfe einzustellen. In dem Film sollte Garbo eine
Durchschnittsfrau spielen. Da die Dreharbeiten
begannen, bevor das Drehbuch fertig war, wurden viele
Einstellungen wiederholt, aber nichts konnte diesen
Film mehr retten. / Garbo attend que l'on mesure sa
distance à la caméra. Ni les retouches au scénario, ni les
innombrables prises ne parviendront à sauver ce film,
qui tente de présenter la star comme une femme
ordinaire.

*"Tomorrow I go to work with a lot of people who
are dead. It's so sad. I'm an onlooker."*
Greta Garbo to Cecil Beaton

*„Morgen werde ich mit vielen Leuten arbeiten, die
tot sind. Es ist so traurig. Ich bin eine Zuschauerin."*
Greta Garbo zu Cecil Beaton

*« Demain, je vais travailler avec beaucoup de gens
qui sont morts. C'est vraiment triste. Je suis une
spectatrice. »*
Greta Garbo à Cecil Beaton

ON THE SET OF 'TWO-FACED WOMAN' (1941)
A prop man resets the table between takes. The film
was condemned by the Catholic Legion of Decency
because of its "immoral and unchristian attitude
towards marriage and its obligations, [and] suggestive
dresses." / Ein Requisiteur richtet den Tisch zwischen
zwei Takes. Die katholische „Anstandsliga" verurteilte
den Film wegen seiner „unmoralischen und
unchristlichen Einstellung zur Ehe und ihren
Verpflichtungen [und] der anzüglichen Kleider". /
Un accessoiriste remet la table entre les prises. Ce film
sera condamné par la ligue de vertu en raison de son
« attitude immorale et peu chrétienne à l'égard du
mariage et de ses obligations, [ainsi que de] ses tenues
suggestives ».

"I never said 'I want to be alone.' I said, 'I want to be left alone' and there is all the difference."
Greta Garbo

„Ich habe nie gesagt: ‚Ich will allein sein.' Ich sagte: ‚Ich will allein gelassen werden' – das ist ein Riesenunterschied."
Greta Garbo

« Je n'ai jamais dit "Laissez-moi seule". J'ai dit "Laissez-moi tranquille", et c'est là toute la différence. »
Greta Garbo

PORTRAIT FOR 'TWO-FACED WOMAN' (1941)
Garbo's last film was made when she was just 36 years old, although she had intermittent projects to make new films until 1950. David Niven asked her why she gave up. Garbo: "I had made enough faces." / Garbo drehte ihren letzten Film im Alter von nur 36 Jahren, obwohl sie bis 1950 erfolglos versuchte, weitere Filmrollen zu bekommen. David Niven fragte sie, warum sie schließlich aufgegeben habe. Garbo: „Ich hatte genug Grimassen geschnitten." / Garbo tourne son dernier film à l'âge de 36 ans, bien qu'elle tente en vain de relancer sa carrière jusqu'en 1950. Lorsque David Niven lui demande pourquoi elle a abandonné, elle répond : « J'avais assez fait de grimaces. »

COVER OF 'MOTION PICTURE' (DECEMBER 1927)

Motion Picture

DECEMBER | 25 CENTS

Greta Garbo

MERLAND
STONE

Read THE Romance of the Movies -- By Benj. B. Hampton

3
CHRONOLOGY

CHRONOLOGIE

CHRONOLOGIE

CHRONOLOGY

18 September 1905 Birth of Greta Lovisa Gustafsson, third daughter of Karl Albert Gustafsson and Anna Karlsson, in Stockholm, Sweden.

1921 Plays in publicity film *How Not to Dress*.

1922 Appears in publicity film for bakery, *Our Daily Bread*. Plays female lead in *Luffar-Petter (Peter the Tramp)*. September: Awarded scholarship to Royal Dramatic Theatre Academy.

1924 10 & 17 March: Premieres of two parts of *Gösta Berlings saga (The Atonement of Gosta Berling)*. November: Louis B. Mayer sees the film in Germany, meets Garbo and proposes three-year contract.

1925 18 May: Berlin and Paris premieres of *Die freudlose Gasse (The Joyless Street)*. 10 September: Stiller and Garbo arrive in Los Angeles. 27 September: Garbo begins shooting *The Torrent*.

1926 21 February: Release of *The Torrent* is a triumphant launch for Garbo. 22 April: Garbo learns of death of her sister Alva. 29 April: Stiller removed from direction of *The Temptress*. 3 May: Fred Niblo takes over direction. 13 August: Refuses to go to studio, so is dismissed from *Flesh and the Devil*. Returns to work and meets John Gilbert, with whom she begins a major love affair. 10 October: Release of *The Temptress*. 13 October: On strike for a better salary.

1927 9 January: Release of *Flesh and the Devil*. 11 April: Commences work on *Anna Karenina* but becomes sick. May: Resumes as *Love*, with director Edmund Goulding and John Gilbert as new leading man. November: Stiller returns to Stockholm. 29 November: Release of *Love*.

1928 14 January: Release of *The Divine Woman*. 4 August: Release of *The Mysterious Lady*. 8 November: Death of Stiller. 5 December: Garbo suspended because she sails for Stockholm.

1929 19 January: Release of *A Woman of Affairs*. 26 March: Arrives back in California. 30 March:

Release of *Wild Orchids*. 29 July: Release of *The Single Standard*. 15 November: Release of *The Kiss*.

1930 22 January: LA premiere of *Anna Christie*. 22 August: Release of *Romance*.

1931 6 February: Release of *Inspiration*. 16 October: Release of *Susan Lenox (Her Fall and Rise)*. 31 December: Release of *Mata Hari*.

1932 12 April: Release of *Grand Hotel*. 2 June: Release of *As You Desire Me*. 29 July: Sails for Sweden.

1933 30 April: Returns to Hollywood. 26 December: Release of *Queen Christina*.

7 December 1934 Premiere of *The Painted Veil*.

1935 30 August: Premiere of *Anna Karenina*; Garbo visits Sweden.

1936 9 January: Death of John Gilbert. 16 September: Death of Irving Thalberg, MGM executive who guided Garbo's career.

1937 22 January: Release of *Camille*. 4 November: Premiere of *Conquest*. The film loses $1,397,000.

May 1938 Independent Theatre Owners of America lists Garbo as 'box office poison.'

26 October 1939 Premiere of *Ninotchka*.

1941 4 December: Release of *Two-Faced Woman*. 6 December: *Two-Faced Woman* withdrawn because of objections from Legion of Decency and other Catholic organisations. 31 December: Definitive release of *Two-Faced Woman*.

15 April 1990 Dies in New York.

COVER OF 'SCREEN PLAY SECRETS' (JUNE 1930)

Screen Play secrets

JUNE
25c

GRETA GARBO
by Henry Clive

Greta
Garbo
Speaks

WHY STARS SHY AT MOTHERHOOD

SCREEN BOOK
MAGAZINE

10ᶜ

May

Greta Garbo

Ann Harding's Love Affair with Her Ex-Husband

CHRONOLOGIE

18. September 1905 Geburt von Greta Lovisa Gustafsson, der dritten Tochter von Karl Alfred Gustafsson und Anna Lovisa Johansson, in Stockholm, Schweden.

1921 Sie tritt in dem Kaufhaus-Werbefilm *Herr och fru Stockholm* auf.

1922 Auftritt in *Konsum Stockholm Promo*, einem Werbefilm für eine Bäckerei. Sie spielt die weibliche Hauptrolle in *Peter, der Vagabund*. September: Stipendium für die Schauspielschule des Königlichen Dramatischen Theaters.

1924 10. und 17. März: Uraufführungen der beiden Teile von *Gösta Berling*. November: Louis B. Mayer sieht den Film in Deutschland, trifft Garbo und unterbreitet ihr einen Dreijahresvertrag.

1925 18. Mai: Erstaufführungen von *Die freudlose Gasse* in Berlin und Paris. 10. September: Stiller und Garbo treffen in Los Angeles ein. 27. September: Garbo beginnt mit den Dreharbeiten zu *Fluten der Leidenschaft*.

1926 21. Februar: *Fluten der Leidenschaft* kommt in die Kinos und wird zu einer triumphalen US-Premiere für Greta Garbo. 22. April: Garbo erfährt vom Tod ihrer Schwester Alva. 29. April: Stiller wird die Regie des Films *Dämon Weib* entzogen. 3. Mai: Fred Niblo übernimmt die Regie. 13. August: Sie weigert sich, ins Atelier zu kommen und wird von den Dreharbeiten zu *Es war* suspendiert, kehrt dann aber zurück und trifft John Gilbert, mit dem sie eine längere Liebesbeziehung beginnt. 10. Oktober: *Dämon Weib* kommt in die Kinos. 13. Oktober: Sie streikt für eine höhere Gage.

1927 9. Januar: Kinopremiere von *Es war*. 11. April: Beginn mit der Arbeit an *Anna Karenina*, wird aber krank. Mai: Setzt unter der Regie von Edmund Goulding die Arbeit an dem Film fort, in dem nun John Gilbert die männliche Hauptrolle spielt. November: Stiller kehrt nach Stockholm zurück. 29. November: *Anna Karenina* kommt in die Kinos.

1928 14. Januar: Kinopremiere von *Das göttliche Weib*. 4. August: *Der Krieg im Dunkel* kommt in die Kinos. 8. November: Stiller stirbt. 5. Dezember: Garbo wird suspendiert, weil sie nach Stockholm reist.

1929 19. Januar: *Eine schamlose Frau* kommt in die Kinos. 26. März: Sie kehrt nach Kalifornien zurück. 30. März: *Wilde Orchideen* kommt in die Kinos. 29. Juli: Kinopremiere von *Unsichtbare Fesseln*. 15. November: *Der Kuß* kommt in die Kinos.

1930 22. Januar: *Anna Christie* feiert Premiere in Los Angeles. 22. August: *Romanze* kommt in die Kinos.

1931 Kinopremieren: 6. Februar: *Yvonne*; 16. Oktober: *Helgas Fall und Aufstieg*; 31. Dezember: *Mata Hari*.

1932 12. April: *Menschen im Hotel* kommt in die Kinos. 2. Juni: Premiere von *Wie du mich willst*. 29. Juli: Reist nach Schweden.

1933 30. April: Kehrt nach Hollywood zurück. 26. Dezember: *Königin Christine* kommt in die Kinos.

7. Dezember 1934 Uraufführung von *Der bunte Schleier*.

1935 30. August: Uraufführung von *Anna Karenina*; Garbo besucht Schweden.

1936 9. Januar: John Gilbert stirbt. 16. September: Produzent Irving Thalberg, der bei MGM über Garbos Karriere wachte, stirbt.

1937 22. Januar: *Die Kameliendame* kommt in die Kinos. 4. November: Uraufführung von *Maria Walewska*. Der Film macht 1.397.000 US-Dollar Verlust.

Mai 1938 Der Verband der unabhängigen Lichtspielhausbesitzer Amerikas brandmarkt Garbo als „Kassengift".

26. Oktober 1939 Uraufführung von *Ninotschka*.

1941 4. Dezember: *Die Frau mit den zwei Gesichtern* kommt in die Kinos. 6. Dezember: *Die Frau mit den zwei Gesichtern* wird aufgrund von Einwänden der „Anstandsliga" und anderer katholischer Organisationen aus dem Verleih genommen. 31. Dezember: *Die Frau mit den zwei Gesichtern* kommt zum zweiten Mal in die Kinos.

15. April 1990 Garbo stirbt in New York.

COVER OF 'SCREEN BOOK' (MAY 1934)

CHRONOLOGIE

18 septembre 1905 Naissance à Stockholm, en Suède, de Greta Lovisa Gustafsson, troisième fille de Karl Albert Gustafsson et d'Anna Lovisa Johansson.

1921 Joue dans un film publicitaire pour les magasins Konsum Stockholm.

1922 Apparaît dans un film publicitaire pour un fabriquant de pain. Interprète le premier rôle féminin dans *Pierre le vagabond*. Septembre : obtient une bourse à l'Académie royale d'art dramatique de Stockholm.

1924 10 et 17 mars : premières des deux parties de *La Légende de Gösta Berling*. Novembre : Louis B. Mayer voit le film en Allemagne, rencontre Garbo et lui propose un contrat de trois ans.

1925 18 mai : première à Berlin et à Paris de *La Rue sans joie*. 10 septembre : Stiller et Garbo arrivent à Los Angeles. 27 septembre : Garbo entame le tournage du *Torrent*.

1926 21 février : sortie du *Torrent* et début triomphal pour Garbo. 22 avril : Garbo apprend le décès de sa sœur Alva. 29 avril : Stiller se voit retirer la réalisation de *La Tentatrice*. 3 mai : Fred Niblo prend le relais. 13 août : Garbo, qui refuse d'entrer en studio, est suspendue de son rôle dans *La Chair et le Diable*. Lorsqu'elle reprend le travail, elle rencontre John Gilbert, avec qui elle entame une grande histoire d'amour. 10 octobre : sortie de *La Tentatrice*. 13 octobre : fait grève pour obtenir une augmentation.

1927 9 janvier : sortie de *La Chair et le Diable*. 11 avril : débute le tournage d'*Anna Karénine*, mais tombe malade. Mai : reprend le tournage avec le réalisateur Edmund Goulding et John Gilbert comme partenaire. Novembre : Stiller rentre à Stockholm. 29 novembre : sortie d'*Anna Karénine*.

1928 14 janvier : sortie d'*Une femme divine*. 4 août : sortie de *La Belle Ténébreuse*. 8 novembre : décès de Stiller. 5 décembre : Garbo part pour Stockholm.

1929 19 janvier : sortie d'*Intrigues*. 26 mars : retour en Californie. 30 mars : sortie de *Terre de volupté*. 29 juillet : sortie du *Droit d'aimer*. 15 novembre : sortie du *Baiser*.

1930 22 janvier : première d'*Anna Christie* à Los Angeles. 22 août : sortie de *Romance*.

1931 6 février : sortie de *L'Inspiratrice*. 16 octobre : sortie de *La Courtisane*. 31 décembre : sortie de *Mata Hari*.

1932 12 avril : sortie de *Grand Hôtel*. 2 juin : sortie de *Comme tu me veux*. 29 juillet : repart pour la Suède.

1933 30 avril : retour à Hollywood. 26 décembre : sortie de *La Reine Christine*.

7 décembre 1934 Première du *Voile des illusions*.

1935 30 août : première d'*Anna Karénine*. Voyage en Suède.

1936 9 janvier : décès de John Gilbert. 16 septembre : décès d'Irving Thalberg, producteur de la MGM qui a guidé la carrière de Garbo.

1937 22 janvier : sortie du *Roman de Marguerite Gautier*. 4 novembre : première de *Marie Walewska*. Le film perd plus d'un million de dollars.

Mai 1938 Les exploitants de salles indépendants font figurer Garbo sur la liste des « poisons du box-office ».

26 octobre 1939 Première de *Ninotchka*.

1941 4 décembre : sortie de *La Femme aux deux visages*. 6 décembre : *La Femme aux deux visages* est retiré des salles suite aux objections de la ligue de vertu et autres organisations catholiques. 31 décembre : sortie définitive de *La Femme aux deux visages*.

15 avril 1990 Greta Garbo décède à New York.

COVER OF 'PHOTOPLAY' (JANUARY 1933)

The NEWS and FASHION MAGAZINE of the SCREEN

PHOTOPLAY

JANUARY

25 CENTS
30 Cents in Canada

Earl Christy

GRETA
GARBO

The High Price of Screen Love-making

Is Dietrich Through?

4

FILMOGRAPHY

FILMOGRAFIE

FILMOGRAPHIE

**Silent Films in Europe/Stummfilme in Europa/
Films muets en Europe**

**Herr och fru Stockholm (eng. 'Mr. and Mrs.
Stockholm', 1921)**
Director/Regie/réalisation: Kapten Ragnar Ring.

En lyckoriddare (eng. 'A Fortune Hunter', 1921)
Maid/Dienstmädchen/servante.
Director/Regie/réalisation: John W. Brunius.

**Konsum Stockholm Promo (eng. 'Our Daily Bread',
1921)**
Director/Regie/réalisation: Kapten Ragnar
Ring.

**Luffar-Petter (eng. 'Peter the Tramp', dt. *Peter, der
Vagabund*, fr. *Pierre le vagabond*, 1922)**
Greta. Director/Regie/réalisation: Erik A. Petschler.

**Gösta Berlings saga (eng. 'The Atonement of Gosta
Berling', dt. *Gösta Berling*, fr. *La Légende de Gösta
Berling*, 1924)**
Elisabeth Dohna. Director/Regie/réalisation: Mauritz
Stiller.

**Die freudlose Gasse (eng. 'The Joyless Street',
fr. *La Rue sans joie*, 1925)**
Greta Rumfort. Director/Regie/réalisation: G. W.
Pabst.

**Silent Films in USA (MGM)/Stummfilme in den
USA (MGM)/Films muets aux États-Unis (MGM)**

**The Torrent (dt. *Fluten der Leidenschaft*,
fr. *Le Torrent*, 1926)**
Leonora Moreno, aka La Brunna.
Director/Regie/réalisation: Monta Bell.

**The Temptress (dt. *Dämon Weib* [aka *Totentanz
der Liebe*], fr. *La Tentatrice*, 1926)**
Elena. Director/Regie/réalisation: Fred Niblo (started
by Mauritz Stiller).

**Flesh and the Devil (dt. *Es war*, fr. *La Chair et le
Diable*, 1927)**
Felicitas. Director/Regie/réalisation: Clarence Brown.

Love (dt. *Anna Karenina*, fr. *Anna Karénine*, 1927)
Anna Karenina/Anna Karenina/Anna Karénine.
Director/Regie/réalisation: Edmund Goulding. (An
initial project for Anna Karenina, to be directed by
Dmitri Buchowetski, was abandoned./Das frühere
Vorhaben einer Verfilmung von Anna Karénina unter
der Regie von Dmitri Buchowetski wurde
aufgegeben./Le projet initial, sous la réalisation de
Dmitri Buchowetski, fut abandonné.)

**The Divine Woman (dt. *Das göttliche Weib* [aka
Der große Star/*Die schönste Frau von Paris*],
fr. *Une femme divine*, 1928)**
Marianne. Director/Regie/réalisation: Victor Sjöström
(Seastrom).

**The Mysterious Lady (dt. *Der Krieg im Dunkel* [aka
Die Dame von Loge 13], fr. *La Belle Ténébreuse*,
1928)**
Tania Fedorova. Director/Regie/réalisation: Fred
Niblo.

**A Woman of Affairs (dt. *Eine schamlose Frau* [aka
Herrin der Liebe], fr. *Intrigues*, 1928)**
Diana Merrick Furness. Director/Regie/réalisation:
Clarence Brown. Released with Movietone

synchronised music and sound effects./Kam mit Movietone-Synchronmusik und -toneffekten in die Kinos./Bande-son synchronisée grâce au procédé Movietone.

Wild Orchids (dt. *Wilde Orchideen*, fr. *Terre de volupté*, 1929)
Lillie Sterling. Director/Regie/réalisation: Sidney A. Franklin. Released with Movietone synchronised music and sound effects./Kam mit dem Movietone-System in die Kinos./Bande-son synchronisée grâce au procédé Movietone.

A Man's Man (fr. *Un homme*, 1929)
Cameo/Cameo-Auftritt (Archivmaterial)/brève apparition. Director/Regie/réalisation: James Cruze. Released with Movietone synchronised music and sound effects./Kam mit dem Movietone-System in die Kinos./Bande-son synchronisée grâce au procédé Movietone.

The Single Standard (dt. *Unsichtbare Fesseln*, fr. *Le Droit d'aimer*, 1929)
Arden Stuart Hewlett. Director/Regie/réalisation: John S. Robertson. Released with Movietone synchronised music and sound effects./Kam mit dem Movietone-System in die Kinos./Bande-son synchronisée grâce au procédé Movietone.

The Kiss (dt. *Der Kuß*, fr. *Le Baiser*, 1929)
Irene Guarry. Director/Regie/réalisation: Jacques Feyder. Released with Movietone synchronised music and sound effects./Kam mit dem Movietone-System in die Kinos./Bande-son synchronisée grâce au procédé Movietone.

Talking Pictures/Tonfilme/Films parlants

Anna Christie (1930)
Anna Christie. Director/Regie/réalisation: Clarence Brown.

Anna Christie (German version/deutsche Fassung/version allemande, 1930)
Anna Christie. Director/Regie/réalisation: Jacques Feyder.

Romance (dt. *Romanze*, fr. *Romance*, 1930)
Madame Rita Cavallini. Director/Regie/réalisation: Clarence Brown.

Inspiration (dt. *Yvonne*, fr. *L'Inspiratrice*, 1931)
Yvonne Valbret. Director/Regie/réalisation: Clarence Brown.

Susan Lenox (aka 'Her Fall and Rise', dt. *Helgas Fall und Aufstieg*, fr. *La Courtisane*, 1931)
Susan Lenox. Director/Regie/réalisation: Robert Z. Leonard.

Mata Hari (1931)
Mata Hari. Director/Regie/réalisation: George Fitzmaurice.

Grand Hotel (dt. *Menschen im Hotel*, fr. *Grand Hôtel*, 1932)
Grusinskaya. Director/Regie/réalisation: Edmund Goulding.

As You Desire Me (dt. *Wie du mich willst*, fr. *Comme tu me veux*, 1932)
Zara. Director/Regie/réalisation: George Fitzmaurice.

Queen Christina (dt. *Königin Christine*, fr. *La Reine Christine*, 1933)
Queen Christina/Königin Kristina/la reine Christine. Director/Regie/réalisation: Rouben Mamoulian.

The Painted Veil (dt. *Der bunte Schleier*, fr. *Le Voile des illusions*, 1934)
Katrin Koerber Fane. Director/Regie/réalisation: Richard Boleslawski.

Garbo

SMILES!

BRIDGEPORT SMILES!
COLUMBUS SMILES!
NEW HAVEN SMILES!
NORFOLK SMILES!
READING SMILES!
RICHMOND SMILES!
SPRINGFIELD SMILES!
WORCESTER SMILES!
NASHVILLE SMILES!
INDIANAPOLIS SMILES!
WASHINGTON SMILES!
ROCHESTER SMILES!
LOUISVILLE SMILES!

**Get ready to join the GARBO
SMILE that's spreading**
from **Coast to Coast!**

Anna Karenina (fr. *Anna Karénine*, 1935)
Anna Karenina/Anna Karénine.
Director/Regie/réalisation: Clarence Brown.

Camille (dt. *Die Kameliendame*, fr. *Le Roman de Marguerite Gautier*, 1936)
Marguerite Gautier. Director/Regie/réalisation: George Cukor.

Conquest (dt. *Maria Walewska* [aka *Marie Walewska*], fr. *Marie Walewska*, 1937)
Countess Marie Walewska/Gräfin Marie Walewska/la comtesse Marie Walewska.
Director/Regie/réalisation: Clarence Brown.

Ninotchka (dt. *Ninotschka*, 1939)
Ninotchka/Ninotschka (Nina Ivanovna Yakushova).
Director/Regie/réalisation: Ernst Lubitsch.

Two-Faced Woman (dt. *Die Frau mit den zwei Gesichtern*, fr. *La Femme aux deux visages*, 1941)
Karin Borg Blake. Director/Regie/réalisation: George Cukor.

BIBLIOGRAPHY

Acosta, Mercedes de: *Here Lies the Heart.* Reynal, 1960.
Bainbridge, John: *Garbo.* Doubleday, 1955.
Beaton, Cecil: *Memoirs of the 40s.* McGraw Hill, 1972.
Beaton, Cecil: *The Wandering Years. Diaries: 1922-1939.* Little, Brown, 1961.
Behrman, S.N.: *People in a Diary: A Memoir.* Little, Brown, 1972.
Billquist, Fritiof: *Garbo.* G.P. Putnam's, 1960.
Broman, Sven: *Conversations with Greta Garbo.* Viking Press, 1992.
Broman, Sven: *Garbo on Garbo.* London: Bloomsbury, 1992.
Broman, Sven & Sands, Frederick: *The Divine Garbo.* Sidgwick & Jackson, 1969.
Brownlow, Kevin: *The Parade's Gone By.* Ballantine, Secker & Warburg, 1968.
Bull, Clarence Sinclair & Lee, Raymond: *Faces of Hollywood.* A. S. Barnes, 1968.
Conway, Michael & McGregor, Dion & Ricci, Mark: *The Films of Greta Garbo.* Bonanza Books, 1965.
Crowther, Bosley: *The Lion's Share.* E.P. Dutton, 1957.
Dance, Robert & Reisfield, Scott: *Garbo, portraits d'une légende.* Flammarion, 2005.
Durgnat, Raymond & Kobal, John: *Greta Garbo.* Dutton Vista, 1965.
Fountain, Leatrice Gilbert with Maxim, John R.: *Dark Star.* St. Martin's Press, 1985.
Gronowicz, Antoni: *Garbo: Her Story.* Simon & Schuster, 1990.
Haining, Peter: *The Legend of Garbo.* W.H. Allen, 1990.

Hamann, G.D.: *Greta Garbo in the 30s.* Filming Today Press, 2003.
Kennedy, Matthew: *Edmund Goulding's Dark Victory: Hollywood's Genius Bad Boy.* University of Wisconsin Press, 2004.
Lacouture, Jean: *Greta Garbo, la dame aux caméras.* Levi/Seuil, 1999.
Laing, E.E.: *Greta Garbo: The Story of a Specialist.* J. Gifford, 1946.
Meyer-Stabley, Bertrand: *La véritable Greta Garbo.* Pygmalion, 2005.
Palmborg, Rilla Page: *The Private Life of Greta Garbo.* Doubleday, 1931.
Paris, Barry: *Garbo: A Biography.* Alfred A. Knopf, 1995.
Payne, Robert: *The Great Garbo.* Praeger, 1976.
Pensel, Hans: *Seastrom and Stiller in Hollywood: Two Swedish Directors in Silent American Films, 1923-1930.* Vantage Press, 1969.
Pepper, Terence & Kobal, John: *The Man Who Shot Garbo.* Simon & Schuster, 1989.
Swenson, Karen: *Greta Garbo: A Life Apart.* Scribner, 1997.
Vickers, Hugo: *Loving Garbo: The Story of Greta Garbo, Cecil Beaton, and Mercedes de Acosta.* Random House, 1994.
Viertel, Salka: *The Kindness of Strangers.* Holt, Rinehart, & Winston, 1969.
Walker, Alexander: *Garbo: A Portrait.* Macmillan, 1980.
Zierold, Norman: *Garbo.* Stein and Day, 1969.

IMPRINT

© 2007 TASCHEN GmbH
Hohenzollernring 53, D-50672 Köln
www.taschen.com

Editor/Picture Research/Layout: Paul Duncan/Wordsmith Solutions
Editorial Coordination: Martin Holz, Cologne
Production Coordination: Nadia Najm and Horst Neuzner, Cologne
German translation: Thomas J. Kinne, Nauheim
French translation: Anne Le Bot, Paris
Multilingual production: www.arnaudbriand.com, Paris
Typeface Design: Sense/Net, Andy Disl and Birgit Reber, Cologne

Printed in Italy
ISBN 978-3-8228-2209-8

To stay informed about upcoming TASCHEN titles, please request our magazine at www.taschen.com/magazine or write to TASCHEN, Hohenzollernring 53, D-50672 Cologne, Germany, contact@taschen.com, Fax: +49-221-254919. We will be happy to send you a free copy of our magazine which is filled with information about all of our books.